Sarah Bernhardt
and Her World

Joanna Richardson

Sarah Bernhardt
and Her World

G. P. Putnam's Sons
New York

Designed by John Wallis
House editor Esther Jagger
Picture editor Julia Brown

SBN: 399-11887-X
Library of Congress Catalog Card Number: 76-29164

Printed in England

Contents

Introduction   7

1   First Performance   13

2   The Flowering of Dreams   28

3   Sarah the Conqueror   74

4   A Great Institution·   154

5   The Stricken Queen   182

6   Final Offering   206

7   Curtain Call   218

Select Bibliography   225

Acknowledgments   227

Index   229

Introduction

'MADAME BERNHARDT has had an adventurous life, which is no business, and not much interest of ours.' The comment was made by a woman writer in 1897. It was acid, prudish and envious. It was also unwise. For adventurous lives have perennial fascination. We enjoy their fairy-tale quality. We revel in the escape which they offer us from the everyday world. And, more important, we may learn from them. The lives of celebrated people give us an insight into human nature; they often show what may be achieved not merely by talent, or even genius, but by resolution. 'You ask me my theory of life,' said Sarah Bernhardt, once. 'It is represented by the word *will*.' In a life of nearly eighty years, a career of more than sixty, and in an age which hardly approved of the 'liberation' of women, she showed, above all, what indomitable will could accomplish.

Sarah Bernhardt became an actress almost by accident; but she was a superb professional. She took infinite pains with every aspect of the dramatic art. She learned her technique not only from her teachers at the Conservatoire, but from her colleagues, from her own triumphs and mistakes, from her wide and vigilant observation of life. She could so identify herself with any part that her fury on stage struck terror into the most placid audience, and her pathos touched Queen Victoria. She burst into fame when, at twenty-five, she played the part of a minstrel boy; she earned a triumph when, at fifty-six, she took the part of another boy: Napoleon's son, l'Aiglon. She could also be the most seductive among women. She conquered a world of admirers, and among them were the Prince of Wales (the future Edward VII), and Napoleon III. Victor Hugo knelt before her. Théophile Gautier sang her praises. Ellen Terry, Burne-Jones and Max Beerbohm, C. B. Cochran, Colette and Clemenceau: the list of Sarah's worshippers is glittering, and it is endless. Sarah was photographed once with the Edwardian beauty, Lily Langtry. The camera recorded Mrs Langtry, a matronly and well-upholstered figure, and Sarah, willowy, in velvet, with a world of mystery in her eyes. In that photograph, perhaps, we may find a hint of her enchantment. She was not conventionally beautiful, but she remained all women in one. She kept this intense femininity to the end of her long life. She owed it not only to her physical appearance, to velvet and chinchilla, to the aura of perfume which hung about her. Nor did she owe it only to her powers as an actress. Her feminine magic was, above all, a quality of spirit.

9

She was, indeed, more than a woman: she was a symbol of woman-hood, a symbol of beauty. And so she inspired not only the poets who wrote for her, but the artists who painted her. The Sarah Bernhardt reflected in the posters of Alphonse Mucha created a new beauty of her own; she set a style of beauty for *fin de siècle* France. And yet, of all her endowments, her voice was the most magical. 'There is more than gold in it,' wrote Lytton Strachey. 'There is thunder and lightning, heaven and hell.' As a girl, she could tame a hostile audience in a Paris theatre simply by the enchantment of her voice. As an old woman, on a bleak November afternoon, in the undramatic setting of the Ritz Hotel in Paris, she could, without props or footlights, without resplendent robes or jewels, recite a poem by Victor Hugo and move a sober audience to tears. Sarah Bernhardt was a great actress, and, perhaps, an actress of genius. She had transcendent personal magic.

Such magic, of course, had brought her a long procession of lovers: actors and artists, poets and princes. By one of her early lovers, Henri, Prince de Ligne, she had her only child, her son, Maurice, who remained the real and permanent love of her life. She married once, disastrously; but perhaps she was not made for marriage. For Sarah, who could play Hamlet and Lady Macbeth, l'Aiglon and la Dame aux camélias, was in a sense both masculine and feminine. She inspired adoration in men and women. Men would fight duels for her sake, women would follow her across the world. But adoration is not love; and lasting, real and ordinary love eluded her. Sarah longed for faithful affection; she was a steadfast friend. But – except in her love for her son – she had no still centre.

And so she was free to lead a flamboyant, eccentric, private life. Her delight in magnificent dress and outrageous conduct, her lovers, her quarrels, her latest escapade were the daily gossip of France. Her vitality was endless, her activities manifold: she was sculptor, critic, author, theatre-manager. She made fortunes, lost them, and made more. She travelled tirelessly. There was, it seemed, no corner of the world so remote that Sarah Bernhardt had not acted there. When some-one, in conversation, mentioned the climate of East Africa, Sarah said: 'I know: I gave a performance in Mombasa.'

Sarah made her début at the Théâtre-Français in 1862 at the height of the Second Empire. She gave her last performance in 1923, when she attempted to film *La Voyante* just before her death. During those sixty-one years her life had been a microcosm of French history. She had known nearly everyone of distinction in France and many who were famous abroad. She had nursed the wounded during the Siege of Paris and recited to the *poilus* during the First World War. She had gone up in a balloon during the Paris Exhibition of 1878 and she had driven across France in a motorcar. She had been taught the art of the stage by Samson, the master of Rachel, and, with her eight films, she had entered the era of the cinema. Few lives have shown such dazzling diversity.

Rachel was the presiding genius in the life of Sarah Bernhardt; and there were similarities between these two Jewish actresses, fighting to achieve pre-eminence. They had both cast themselves, with fervour, into *Phèdre* and *Adrienne Lecouvreur*. They had both astonished the world by the quantity and distinction of their liaisons, by their emotional energy on and off the stage. They had both shown a Jewish devotion to their children and to their parasitic and unworthy families. They had both amazed the world by their triumphal tours abroad. They had both left a challenge and an aura in the theatre.

And yet their achievements were profoundly different. Rachel had been a tragic actress, a supremely magnificent Phèdre, and she had rarely succeeded in modern drama. Sarah had played the plays of the nineteenth and twentieth centuries. Rachel was summed up in the word *tragédienne*, Sarah in the phrase *artiste dramatique*. Rachel had plunged deep, and Sarah had ranged wide over the theatre. It is hard to say that one was greater than the other.

And yet, in following the brief life of Rachel, one becomes aware of a dedicated spirit, of a woman lost in admiration of the works which she interpreted. 'Oh my sweet Racine, it is in your masterpieces that I recognise the heart of woman! I shape my own to your noble poetry. If the lyre of my soul does not always weep with your harmonies divine, it is that admiration leaves my whole being in ecstasy.' Could Sarah have written as much of any poet, of any dramatist she knew?

The whole of her career suggests that it was impossible. When Pierre Louÿs, the novelist and poet, cried: 'Always Sarah, Sarah ...', he unconsciously summed up her character and career. When Francisque Sarcey, the critic, explained: 'Whatever disguise she puts on, she is always Sarah,' he merely confirmed Louÿs' words. And when the English critic observed that Sarah was a peerless institution, he came as close as anyone to the heart of the matter.

For despite the quantity of parts she played, despite the power and variety of her gifts, despite her all-absorbing, progressive love of her art, Sarah's greatest achievement was her personal *mise-en-scène*, the part of Sarah Bernhardt. Her interests were vivid and many; her friendships and her passions were lasting and strong; but she always saw herself as the leading actress in the grandiose performance of life. She was as great an egoist as Napoleon. Like the Emperor, she proved enough to hold a world in fee, to inspire a cult and a legend. She affirmed her virtues, she did not seek to hide her weaknesses, she would tell enquiring journalists the wildest myths: not so much, one feels, to hide her real self from a prying world, as to set the world talking, once again, of Sarah.

One cannot deny that she herself was the first high priestess of the Bernhardt legend. One cannot deny that her exhibitionism sometimes led her astray. Yet she lived so intensely, so constantly, in fact and in fiction, that she seemed to all men an epitome of all things.

That is why Sarah Bernhardt's life must be our concern. There remains a fraction of truth in Edmond de Goncourt's suggestion: 'The life of Mme Sarah Bernhardt may prove the greatest marvel of the nineteenth century.'

1
First
Performance

Sarah Bernhardt, at the age of eight, with her mother.

ON 23 OCTOBER 1844, at an undistinguished address in Paris –
22, rue de la Michodière – a girl of sixteen gave birth to a
daughter. There was no rejoicing at the event. Indeed, there
was probably regret, because the child was illegitimate and
its existence might impede the mother's career. Judith Van Hard
earned her living as a courtesan. Sarah-Marie-Henriette was her
daughter by Édouard Bernhardt.

Judith Van Hard was Jewish, and she came from Haarlem. She was
'ravishingly beautiful,' Sarah wrote long afterwards, 'like a Madonna,
with her golden hair'. As for Édouard Bernhardt, his daughter was to
recall him (glorified, perhaps, by memory) as imposing and divinely
handsome. He came of a good Roman Catholic family in Le Havre;
he had abandoned his lawyer's career to travel about the world. But
from time to time, like some homing bird, he would return to France
to enchant her.

Judith Van Hard did not compensate Sarah for his absence. She soon
deposited the unwanted baby with Édouard Bernhardt's old nurse, a
buxom Breton, who was married to a farmer near Quimperlé. Sarah
long remembered the little white cottage with a low thatched roof on
which wallflowers grew. She remained there for the early years of her
life; and there, it seems, she developed her love for limitless landscapes.
'I adore the sea and the wild open spaces,' she was to write, 'but I
do not like mountains, or forests. Mountains crush me. Forests stifle
me. Whatever happens, I must have a boundless horizon, and a sky
in which I can lose all my dreams.'

Very suddenly the décor of Sarah's childhood changed. Judith Van
Hard descended on the cottage and took her with the nurse and the
nurse's ailing husband to Paris. She installed them in a little house in
a garden full of dahlias, at Neuilly on the banks of the Seine. But, as
Sarah was to write: 'My mother adored travelling. She would flit from
Spain to England; from London to Paris; from Paris to Berlin. From
there she would go to Christiania; then come back and kiss me and
set off again for Holland, her native country.' Her constant travels were
explained by her series of liaisons. Once she had left her daughter at
Neuilly, she was off again. She acknowledged her maternity by random
presents of money, by occasional parcels of sweets and toys. She did
not trouble to leave an address. When the nurse's husband died, the
nurse re-married and went to live with her new spouse, a Parisian con-

cierge. She simply took the five-year-old child to her new home over the courtyard door of 65, rue de Provence. No doubt she did her best to look after Édouard Bernhardt's daughter; but she gave her a room without a window. Sarah was overcome by despair. She refused to eat, and she would have died (so she said in her memoirs) had it not been for a chance event which might have come from a romantic novel. One day she was playing in the courtyard. She glanced up to see Tante Rosine, her mother's sister, who happened to be looking for an apartment.

I uttered a cry of delight and of deliverance [remembered Sarah]. 'Tante Rosine! Tante Rosine!' ... I buried my face in her furs: I shuddered; I sobbed; I laughed; I tore her long lace sleeves ....

I caught hold of my aunt, who smelt so sweet, ... so sweet, and I wouldn't let her go. She promised to come and fetch me next day; ... but I wanted to set off, with my nurse, at once. My aunt gently stroked my hair ....

Frivolous, and tender, and cajoling, and without love, she spoke sweet words to me; she stroked me with her gloved hands. ...

Then Sarah was led upstairs, in tears, to watch the carriage depart.

Perhaps she had already learned to mistrust the promises of adults. Perhaps she was simply desperate and wanted attention – or perhaps she really wanted to end her life. On a dramatic impulse she jumped out of the window. Her arm was fractured in two places and her knee-cap was broken.

She woke up in a large bed, in a room that was full of sunshine. Judith Van Hard was for once conscientious, and hastened to look after her; and Sarah found herself surrounded by solicitous aunts and cousins. It took her, so she said, two years to recover from her fall.

When Sarah was seven years old, and her mother was expecting another child, she was bundled off to a pension at Auteuil. She was not unhappy there: indeed she settled down cheerfully to her new and welcome independence. She grew accustomed to the routine. Suddenly, after two years, it was broken. On her father's orders, Tante Rosine arrived to take her away. Sarah fought for two hours to escape her. She fled to the garden and climbed the trees; she threw herself in the pond (it happened to be full of mud, not water). Exhausted, sobbing and frustrated, she was finally driven away to the rue de la Chaussée-d'Antin, and put to bed. She was in a fever for three days.

A few weeks later, accompanied by her parents and by a trunk of belongings all marked in scarlet cotton, 's B', she was driven off to the convent of Grand-Champs at Versailles. Édouard Bernhardt promised her that four years hence he would come and fetch her, and take her away on his travels.

Yet another promise was to be broken. She did not see him again. Her mother vanished once more on her errant life, flitting from spa to spa, from boudoir to boudoir. It was Mère Sainte-Sophie, Mother Superior of Grand-Champs, who now guided Sarah's life.

Mère Sainte-Sophie was, naturally enough, the first person for whom the discarded, rootless child felt deep affection. Her kindness, courage and gaiety won Sarah's heart. It was Mère Sainte-Sophie who calmed her when she flew into rages; Mère Sainte-Sophie who roused the finer instincts that her father and mother had failed to encourage. Sarah only wanted some absorbing emotion. It was not surprising that she wanted to stay at the convent for ever. Her mystic tendencies were confirmed by an epoch-making event. Monseigneur Sibour, Archbishop of Paris, arranged to visit Grand-Champs.

The news sent the convent into a turmoil. Mère Sainte-Thérèse wrote a short play in three tableaux for the occasion. When she read *Tobie recouvrant sa vue*, the very reading moved them all to tears. Sarah, trembling with apprehension, waited to hear what part she had been assigned. She was given nothing. Outraged and furious, she created a part for herself: the shepherd's dog. But it was of no avail. She entered for the competition to make the fish's costume; but, alas, her costume was not chosen.

And then, at the dress rehearsal, she was given her chance. The Archangel Raphael collapsed from stage-fright, and declared that she could never say her part. And a triumphant understudy, who had carefully learnt the words, scrambled on to the platform waving a willow branch in her hand, and continued: 'Fear not, Tobias, I will be thy guide . . .'

Sarah Bernhardt was giving her first performance.

At last the day of the visit arrived, and *Tobie recouvrant sa vue* was performed in triumph. Monseigneur Sibour not only gave each child a holy medal, but promised to return in the spring for Sarah's baptism. From that day forward she became more studious, more serene. And then in January 1857, the horrified convent learned how, during a service at Saint-Étienne-du-Mont, a mad priest had murdered Monseigneur Sibour. The news was an acute shock to the sensitive child; her love of mysticism grew stronger than ever.

As the time of her baptism approached she would weep for no apparent reason, and she had irrational fears.

One day, one of my friends dropped my doll, which I had lent her (because I played with a doll until after I was thirteen), and I began to tremble in every limb. I adored the doll, which my father had given me. 'You've broken my doll's head, you beast! You have hurt my father!' I refused to eat. And, that night, I woke up in a cold sweat, wild-eyed, sobbing: 'Papa is dead! Papa is dead!'

Three days later, Maman came to see me in the parlour, and stood me in front of her. 'Darling, I'm going to upset you ... Papa is dead!' 'I know, I know!' And I looked at her in such a way, my mother has often told me, that she feared for my reason.

And then came Sarah's baptism and her first communion. She was pale and thin, wide-eyed, in perpetual ecstasy. It was only when her mother took her off to Cauterets in the Pyrenees that the bustle and excitement of travel and the change of countryside did their work. Her nervousness was overcome; so was her mysticism. For the first time she began to live.

She returned from Cauterets to Grand-Champs, where she stayed for another ten months. Then Judith Van Hard took her back to Paris; and the imposing Mlle de Brabender, who had once been governess to a Russian Grand Duchess, arrived each morning to supervise Sarah's lessons.

What was her future to be? One September morning in 1859, just before her fifteenth birthday, several guests assembled for *déjeuner*: Mlle de Brabender, M. Régis (Sarah's godfather), Tante Rosine, and, finally, an elegant, balding, dark-haired man with a moustache and an imperial, a worldly man in his forties, an imposing man who, within the last decade, had helped to lay the foundations of the Second Empire. He was the current lover of Judith Van Hard, the Emperor's half-brother, the Duc de Morny.

After *déjeuner*, one or two others joined the council to discuss Sarah's future. Sarah was still determined to take the veil. It was the Duc de Morny who ended the deliberations. Perhaps he made the suggestion from genuine percipience. Perhaps he saw it as a convenient way of ridding his mistress of an unwanted daughter. Perhaps he ventured a guess, at random, because he was growing bored. Whatever his motive, he decided Sarah Bernhardt's career. 'You know what to do with the child?' he said. 'Send her to the Conservatoire.'

Sarah felt no longing to enter the theatre. Long ago, when she was very small and walking with her mother in the Tuileries Gardens, she had seen an enormous woman sitting across two seats. Judith Van Hard had told her to remember the woman because she was the great actress Mlle Georges. Sarah had never seen anything so huge, except for elephants, and she had screamed. She had a lifelong horror of obesity. And then, one day, at Grand-Champs, she had seen a woman, dying of consumption, who had come to visit a child at the convent. The woman had sat for a while in the convent gardens. Sœur Appoline had told Sarah that this was Rachel. How could Sarah want to follow that woman, prematurely old, who had only earned the mockeries of the convent children?

But the Duc de Morny had decided that Sarah was to enter the theatre, and that evening in September 1859, with her mother, M. Régis and Mlle de Brabender, she went to see *Britannicus* at the Théâtre-Français. She had not been to the theatre before, except to see the conjuror, Robert-Houdin; and when the chandeliers grew dim, the curtain slowly rose, she thought that she would faint with emotion. It was in fact the curtain of her life that was rising.

And soon the necessary volumes of Corneille and Racine arrived; and Daniel Auber, the composer, Director of the Conservatoire, summoned her to see him. A month later came the entrance examination, and she found herself before an awe-inspiring board of examiners: Auber himself, Jean-Baptiste Provost, the tragedian, and a buxom, outspoken woman in her thirties who studied Sarah mercilessly through her lorgnette: Augustine Brohan. Sitting with them was Joseph-Isidore Samson, a small, benevolent, white-haired man who had been the master of Rachel.

She stood before them, strangely thin and frail, with an unruly aureole of fair hair, a slightly Jewish face dominated by compelling eyes.

One could no more have said that this face was pretty than affirm that it was ugly [wrote the actress Marie Colombier]. . . . It was like one of those unfinished heads which you see in sculptors' studios. The final modelling, the last touch was missing. . . .

19

And yet its unforgettable strangeness did not come from this unfinished quality. It came from the eyes, the very long, superb eyes. The pupils changed colour with the variations of light, with the movements of the face. They were old gold when the child was dreaming, cat's-eye green when she knit her brows in anger, dark blue when she smiled. . . .

Sarah recited La Fontaine's fable, *Les Deux Pigeons*, and her voice already astonished, already conquered.

Sarah Bernhardt was admitted into the Conservatoire. The words '*Mademoiselle, vous êtes admise*,' fell on ears which expected nothing else. Beauvallet and Provost both asked to have her in their class, and Sarah was allowed to choose her master. She disliked Beauvallet's outspoken manner, and she chose Provost. 'I have only one regret,' said Auber. 'It is that your lovely voice is not destined for music.'

Sarah won the second prize for tragedy at her first examination. She took lessons in deportment. Long afterwards, May Agate, who was one of Sarah's pupils, remembered: 'Carriage was a thing of the first importance with Mme Sarah. . . . "May, *tenez-vous droite*," still rings in my ears.' Every morning Judith Van Hard gave Sarah twenty sous for omnibus fares, and every morning Sarah saved the money so that she might return by cab on alternate days. Even now she enjoyed her exits and her entrances. Her favourite class was that of the gentle, courteous Régnier, who taught sincerity of diction. But she learned her grandiose gestures from Provost, her simplicity from Samson, whose favourite maxim was: 'Gesture precedes and prepares for words.' Sarah did not forget the lesson. 'Never shock the spectator', she was to tell May Agate, 'by abruptness of speech or gesture. Register the thought before the action.'

She entered for her second examination with the resolve (for Sarah always hastened to extremes) that if she did not win the first prize for comedy she would renounce the theatre and take the veil. Alas, she did not win the prize. It was a young actress (oddly enough called Marie Lloyd) whom she saw acclaimed as Célimène. The lesson was to serve Sarah Bernhardt throughout her life. Marie Lloyd had won her prize as the incarnation of the coquette. She had realized Molière's ideal. 'I have never forgotten her prize,' Sarah wrote towards the end of her days. 'And whenever I create a part, the character itself appears before me. . . .' When Sarah at the height of her fame was playing Cleopatra, Mrs Patrick Campbell asked why – since the audience would not see

Sarah Bernhardt when she left the Conservatoire.
From a photograph by Nadar.

them – Sarah tinted the palms of her hands. '*I* shall see them,' said Sarah. 'I am doing it for myself. If I catch sight of my hand, it will be the hand of Cleopatra. That will help me.'

She was helped, one must admit, in her early years by the distinguished men who frequented her mother's boudoir. After her second examination it was Camille Doucet, Ministre des Beaux-Arts, and the Duc de Morny, who saw that she entered the Maison de Molière. She was received – and accepted – by M. Thierry, administrator-general of the Théâtre-Français.

Her relationship with the first theatre of France was to be stormy. But for all her vagaries, for all her independence, it remained her spiritual home because it was the temple of her art. It is said that the heir to a great throne, who did not uncover in the foyer, was given a respectful reminder. 'Your Royal Highness,' Sarah murmured, 'you do not take off your crown here – but you bare your head.'

Once Judith Van Hard had signed her daughter's contract with the Comédie-Française, Sarah threw herself into the theatre with the ardour which she had once shown for religion. She determined that if she was to be an actress, she would be an actress of distinction; perhaps already, in her childish heart, she had decided to be the greatest of all actresses.

Unlike her predecessor, Rachel, she started with advantages. Her mother, it is true, lacked the warmth and affection of Mme Félix, and was always glad to dispose of her unwanted daughter. But Judith Van Hard was not a pedlar's wife; she was the mistress of the Duc de Morny. Sarah's destiny had been decided by a duke, it was a duke who had quietly smoothed her way; and, a few days after she had entered the Comédie-Française, Tante Rosine gave a dinner-party that many débutantes would have envied. Morny was there, of course; and so was Comte Alexandre Walewski, the illegitimate son of Napoleon, from the Ministère des Beaux-Arts. So was Rossini. It was Gioacchino Rossini, the composer of *William Tell*, who invited Sarah to recite. It was for Rossini that she declaimed *L'Âme du Purgatoire* by Casimir Delavigne, and it was at Walewski's suggestion, with Rossini as accompanist, that she repeated the poem. The Comte de Kératry, an elegant young hussar, paid her many compliments, and invited her to recite at his mother's. The girl who had left home embarrassed by her first evening dress went home again transformed. Some say that Kératry was the first of her lovers – and perhaps he was indeed the first in the long procession that was to pass through Sarah Bernhardt's life. Many actresses, said Arsène Houssaye, believed that the theatre was a baptism which saved them from original sin.

On 1 September 1862 – more than sixty years before her last appearance – Sarah Bernhardt made her début as Iphigénie.

She took an infinite time to dress; and when the curtain rose she felt faint with apprehension. Provost, tall, grey-haired, paternal, was waiting in the wings to encourage her. It was he who heard Iphigénie's cue and pushed her on to the first stage of France.

She flew to her father, Agamemnon, and clung to him; she hurled herself at her mother, Clytemnestra. She gabbled her part; and, when she came off stage, she fled to her room and feverishly began to undress. She had to be reminded that there were four acts still to come. Sarah conquered her nervousness and returned to the stage; but she was insignificant. 'Mlle Bernhardt, who made her début yesterday in *Iphigénie*, is a tall, pretty young girl,' wrote Francisque Sarcey in *L'Opinion Nationale*. 'The upper part of her face is remarkably fine. She holds herself well and pronounces with perfect clarity. That is all one can say at the moment.'

It is customary at the Théâtre-Français to make three débuts. Sarah made her second in *Valérie*; she made her third as Henriette in *Les Femmes savantes*, and called forth another critical outburst from Sarcey. 'This performance was very poor, and inspires some sad reflections. That Mlle Bernhardt should be inadequate does not matter, for she is beginning; but it is sad that the actors supporting her were not much better than she was. And they are *sociétaires*! They had not many advantages over their young companion except a greater knowledge of the boards; they are to-day what Mlle Bernhardt will be in twenty years' time if she remains at the Comédie-Française.'

Fate decreed that Sarah did not remain there. It was Molière's birthday and as usual the Comédie were to garland his bust on stage. It was the first time that Sarah had attended the ceremony and her youngest sister, Régina, had begged to be taken.

The whole Comédie was assembled in the foyer; the call-boy announced that the ceremony was about to begin, and everyone crowded into the corridor where the busts of the great actors were displayed. In this confusion, Régina trod on Mme Nathalie's train.

23

Mme Nathalie, a stout and pompous *sociétaire*, pushed the child aside, and Régina fell and cut her face. Mlle Sarah Bernhardt boxed Mme Nathalie's ears.

The curtain rose, that night, twenty minutes late. Next morning Mlle Sarah Bernhardt received a summons from the administrator. She was asked to make a formal apology to the offended *sociétaire*. She refused to do so, and resigned.

Sarah's violent break with the Comédie had its natural repercussions in her family life, and there were perpetual reproaches. But the family did not abandon its hopes for Sarah's future. Again the chain of well-wishers set to work; and in May 1863 she duly found herself in the offices of Montigny, Director of the Théâtre du Gymnase. Montigny lectured her briefly on her flight from the Comédie, and promised her many fine parts. Then he drew up her contract, and she signed it.

For the first few months he kept his word. And then, one day, he gave her the part of Princess Dunchinka, 'a Russian princess, with nothing to do but eat and dance all the time', in a play by Raymond Deslandes, *Un Mari qui lance sa femme.*

It was a disappointing part; but Sarah found it more than disappointing. Since she always went to extremes, she decided to give up the theatre; and now that the thought of the convent had faded from her mind, she decided to go into business. A family friend advised her to take a confectioner's shop in the boulevard des Italiens. At the sight of it, Princess Dunchinka renounced the thought of commerce for ever.

It must be admitted that there was a deeper reason for Sarah's vagaries than mere caprice or professional disappointment. Her mother was anxious to be free of an unwanted daughter. More than once she had suggested suitors for Sarah's hand: bourgeois aspirants, of course, for an illegitimate girl could claim no more. Sarah had understandably turned them aside, and she had found herself a lover to fulfil her dreams of romance. By the spring of 1864 she was the mistress of Henri, Prince de Ligne.

He came of one of the oldest families in Belgium; he was young and indubitably handsome. There could be no question of marriage, but in March Sarah was pregnant.

Sarah Bernhardt was not even noticed in the first performance of *Un Mari qui lance sa femme*, except by her mother. 'My poor child, you were ridiculous!' she said. 'You were a great disappointment.'

For all her mother's cutting indifference, Sarah was fond of her, and the comment hurt. No doubt she was suffering, too, from her pregnancy. Next morning, she collected her savings and, snatching the crucifix from her bedroom wall, she was down the stairs and in a cab and on her way to Spain before her mother had drunk her morning coffee. When the news arrived at the Gymnase Montigny simply said: 'May the Devil take her!'

For a fortnight and more Sarah revelled in Spain. She might have settled there if she had not received a telegram from Mme Guérard, her friend and confidante in Paris, telling her that her mother was gravely ill. Sarah promptly took the train for Paris, where Judith Van Hard was recovering from pleurisy.

But the flight to Spain had taught her the delights of independence; and now, as her child was about to be born, she learned that half the dowry bequeathed to her by her father would be given to her immediately. She moved to the rue Duphot with her sister, Régina. A *femme de chambre* was installed, a cook was engaged, and Mme Guérard spent most of her days there. It was at the rue Duphot, on 22 December, that Sarah found a new purpose in life, a new and permanent centre for her affections. She gave birth to Maurice, her son by Henri, Prince de Ligne and her only child.

2
The Flowering of Dreams

'Like an angelic musician by Donatello.'
Sarah Bernhardt in *Le Passant*.

La Biche aux bois was often staged at the Porte-Saint-Martin, and Sarah often went to see the immensely popular *féerie*. But one evening in December 1865, she entered the foyer and encountered an actor whom she knew. 'Here she is !' he cried. 'Here she is ! Our princess, our little *biche aux bois*, here she is ! The god of the theatre has sent her to us !'

The *jeune première* was ill and Sarah had arrived like a *dea ex machina*. In vain she protested. She had heard the words so often that she knew them by heart. She was pushed into the costume of Princesse Désirée. The curtain rose. When it fell, she was offered a three-year contract.

Could she abandon Racine for light entertainment? Before she made her decision, she wrote to Camille Doucet; and M. le Ministre des Beaux-Arts, who treated her like an indulgent father, sent her to see Félix Duquesnel, Director of the Théâtre de l'Odéon. Sarah was charmed by the young and elegant Duquesnel, and she signed yet another contract.

The Odéon became her favourite theatre; the company was happy there, the audience was full of eager students, and Duquesnel was gallant and entertaining. The Prince de Ligne had departed, but Pierre Berton, the handsomest actor in Paris after Mounet-Sully, was wildly enamoured of her. More than once she refused his proposals of marriage, but their liaison lasted over two years; and all their days together, he said long afterwards, were like pages from immortality. How different it seemed at the Odéon from the pompous, parochial world of the Comédie-Française!

Sarah played the wild baroness in *Le Marquis de Villemer*, and Mariette in *François le Champi*, both dramas based on novels by George Sand. During rehearsals she was charmed by George Sand herself, with her wide and dreaming eyes. Prince Napoleon, the Emperor's cousin, better known as Plon-Plon, was devoted to Mme Sand and often came to rehearsals, and the first time Sarah saw him her heart stopped beating, for he so resembled the great Napoleon. George Sand introduced them; and Sarah delighted in his conversation. He was charming to women; he had fascinating manners, and a more than ordinary appreciation of art. The papers were quick to suggest that the lover of Rachel had come to be the lover of Sarah Bernhardt; and it would not be beyond probability.

When Sarah appeared as Anna Damby, in Dumas' *Kean*, she once again

31

Napoleon III, the Empress Eugénie and the Prince Imperial. From a photograph taken in the mid 1860s.

proved the spell of her voice. It was at a moment when feelings ran high among the followers of Dumas and those of the exiled Hugo; and before the curtain rose on the first night of *Kean*, there were tumultuous cries of '*Ruy Blas! Ruy Blas!* Victor Hugo! Victor Hugo!' After an hour Duquesnel decided that the play must begin. It was an alarming audience to face. When Sarah made her appearance in the clinging clothes of 1820, there was a burst of laughter. But Sarah was always inspired by a challenge. Her motto *Quand même* reflected a fixed determination. As a child of nine she had chosen it. She had been dared to jump a ditch which nobody could cross; she had jumped it, and hurt herself badly. But, even as she was carried away, she had cried out in fury: 'Yes, yes, I should do it again, *quand même*, in spite of everything, if they dared me again! And I shall always do what I want to do!' Now she rose to the challenge of the audience at the Théâtre de l'Odéon. When she declared her love for Kean, she received an ovation. 'Her magic voice, her astonishing voice, moved the public,' said *Le Figaro*. 'She tamed them, like a little Orpheus.'

There were moments of triumph in Sarah's life. Yet, by the end of 1868, she found herself approaching twenty-five, and still (apart from her escapades) virtually unknown. She must have reflected bitterly on the destiny of Rachel who, at seventeen, had earned the approval of Mlle Mars and the pontifical praise of Jules Janin: Rachel, who, when barely twenty, had swept aside all prejudice and conquered the English public overnight.

One wonders how long Sarah might have waited for fame had it not been for a young clerk at the Ministry of War by the name of François Coppée. That September he wrote a one-act poetic drama, *Le Passant*.

Silvia, the Venetian courtesan, is growing weary. She longs for young, pure love, and dreams beneath the stars one evening when the wind is warm. There comes a young boy playing a guitar and singing as he passes. Silvia feels her heart touched by new passion; then, seeing his innocence, she feels that she must save him from disillusion. She asks him to go and shows him his road. Zanetto takes his guitar and cloak, and slowly goes into the distance, and the play evaporates rather than ends.

Mlle Agar, Coppée's mistress, heard the play with enthusiasm. She demanded the part of Silvia, and insisted on a young colleague at the Odéon as Zanetto. 'Sarah Bernhardt is charming, and I think she was

32

Sarah Bernhardt: a portrait painted on china in 1880.

Sarah Bernhardt

The author of *Le Passant*:
François Coppée (1842–1908).

born for the part.' Early in January 1869 Coppée watched the dress rehearsal.

What can I say of Agar, so majestically beautiful in her white satin dress with its flowing train?... What can I say of Sarah, then so slim, so svelte! Sarah, whose whole person had the suppleness, the lightness, the grace of a boy? What nobility of gesture, what deep emotion in my Silvia! What rapture, what delight, what youthful folly in my Zanetto! They both recited marvellously, and I took infinite pleasure in the contrast between the enchanting golden voice of Sarah and the moving contralto of Agar. One word must be used to describe the first interpretation of *Le Passant*. It was perfection.

A few days after the first performance the timid young clerk at the Ministry of War, very ignorant of the ways of the world, was introduced by Théophile Gautier, at the request of Princess Mathilde, the high patroness of art, into the sumptuous salons of the rue de Courcelles. He was asked if *Le Passant* might be performed there in the presence of Napoleon III. On 29 April Princess Mathilde gave her annual reception for the Emperor's birthday. After this evening, Agar was received by the Emperor's command in the Comédie-Française. Sarah Bernhardt's sovereign future was assured.

And there was not only a performance at the rue de Courcelles; there

35

Sarah Bernhardt in the title-rôle of *Frou-Frou*, a drawing-room comedy by Henri Meilhac and Ludovic Halévy. A *Vanity Fair* cartoon by Théobald Chartran, 1879.

Princess Mathilde, the Emperor's cousin, patron of the arts.
A painting of her in her studio by her friend Eugène Giraud.

was a performance at the Tuileries. Before the dress-rehearsal, Sarah encountered the Emperor himself.

I liked him much better like this, seen close to, than I did in his portraits [she remembered].... His smile was rather enigmatic. His face was pale....

We arrived [at the Tuileries] to find the Empress sitting in a big armchair. She was wearing a grey dress, and her body seemed as if it were moulded in the fabric.

I found her very pretty – even prettier than she was in her portraits.

The Emperor looked on, benignly, and I made my three curtseys.

Then the Empress spoke, and the charm was gone. The harsh and raucous voice which came from that fair figure gave me an almost physical shock. From that moment, I felt ill at ease with her, in spite of her grace and her benevolence.

When Agar had come, and had been presented, the Empress led us into the great salon where the performance was to take place....

The Prince Imperial arrived – he was then thirteen – and he helped me to arrange the plants....

He was delightful, the young prince, with his splendid eyes....

He was as witty as the Emperor, the Emperor whom people dubbed 'Louis the Imbecile', the Emperor who certainly had the finest, the most subtle, and also the most generous of minds.

On 11 June *Le Moniteur universel* duly reported: 'Yesterday evening there was a dinner at the Tuileries in honour of the Queen of the Netherlands. Prince Napoleon and Princess Clotilde, Princess Mathilde, the Ministers of the Netherlands and Wurtemberg were present. After dinner the artists of the Odéon performed *Le Passant*.'

The Emperor gave Zanetto a bracelet. Zanetto long remembered him with affection.

Napoleon III was not to be Emperor much longer. On 15 July 1870, France embarked on the Franco-Prussian War. Sarah was shaken by the wild scenes she witnessed in Paris, the frenzied singing of *La Marseillaise*, the cries of '*À Berlin! À Berlin!*' The campaign soon proved to be disastrous; the Emperor surrendered to William 1 of Prussia at Sedan. On 4 September the Bonapartes were deposed. The Empress fled to England. The Second Empire was over, and the Republic was proclaimed. But the catastrophic war continued. When the Siege of Paris began, Sarah sent Maurice and his nurse, her mother and her sisters to Le Havre, and she decided to organize a hospital. With the help of Félix Duquesnel, she installed one in the Odéon.

38

THE FLOWERING OF DREAMS

It was not enough to have the theatre. Sarah needed food, and she sent a note to the Prefect of Police. By one of the curious chances in her life, the Prefect was the Comte de Kératry who had admired her once at Tante Rosine's and who, some say, had been the first of her lovers. Kératry, fired by her resolution and, perhaps, by memory, asked her to call at his office at the Tuileries.

The palace was no longer the same [wrote Sarah].... The gentle fragrance left in the air by the passing of elegant women had disappeared. A vague smell of tobacco, greasy clothes and dirty hair hung in the atmosphere.

Oh, the pretty Empress of the French!... That delightful Prince Imperial, I remembered him helping me to arrange the pots of verbena and marguerites, and carrying an enormous pot of rhododendrons which was too heavy for his frail arms....

And, finally, I recalled the Emperor Napoleon III, with his half-closed eyes....

And now the blond Empress had fled, dressed in strange clothes, in the coupé of her American dentist; for it was not even a Frenchman who had the courage

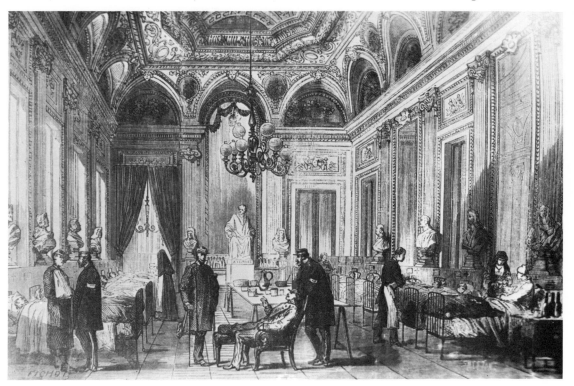

A scene in the Franco-Prussian War, 1870–1:
the military hospital in the Théâtre-Français.

to protect the unhappy woman, it was a foreigner. And the gentle Emperor, with his Utopian dreams, had tried in vain to get himself killed on the battle-field. Two horses killed under him, and not a scratch. And he had surrendered his sword. And we had all wept with rage, with shame and grief when we learned of this surrender. And what courage he must have had, that brave man, to do that deed! He had wanted to save a hundred thousand men, spare a hundred thousand lives, reassure a hundred thousand mothers!

Poor dear Emperor! History will one day do him justice, because he was good and humane, and trusting. Alas, alas, he trusted too much!

Meanwhile, in the autumn of 1870, the Emperor was deposed, and the wounded soldiers waited in the Théâtre de l'Odéon. Kératry gave Sarah ten barrels of red wine, two of brandy, thirty thousand eggs, a hundred bags of coffee, twenty boxes of tea, forty cases of biscuits and a thousand boxes of preserves. His generosity did not end there, for Sarah saw his fur-lined overcoat and promptly commandeered it for a patient. On her second visit she found Kératry hiding his cloth overcoat, for fear that she would take it as well.

Kératry was not her only supporter. 'M. Menier, the great chocolate manufacturer, sent me five hundred pounds of chocolate,' she recorded. 'A friend of mine, a flour-merchant, had given me twenty sacks of flour. . . . Félix Potin, my former neighbour,. . . had answered my appeal and had sent me two barrels of raisins, a hundred tins of sardines, three sacks of rice. . . . From M. de Rothschild I had received two barrels of brandy and a hundred bottles of his wine for the convalescent.' The Dutch Ambassador sent her lint and linen. She needed such munificence. She had sixty beds in the Odéon, and hundreds of wounded passed through her hands. She installed her own cook in the boxes with a cooking range to provide soup and tea. Outside in the street as the siege went on there were pitiful queues for surplus milk and meat.

On 27 December the bombardment of Paris began. The hospital flag on the Odéon served as a target for the Prussian guns, and the patients had to be packed in the rat-infested cellars. They were only transferred when the cellars were flooded.

Clad in her pink bonnet and her little white apron, Sarah herself was now playing one of her finest parts. The war had taught her the smallness of individuals. It helped to tame her conceit, to teach her the importance of patriotism. 'I am French,' she was to say, 'I am French by birth, at heart, in spirit, art and love.' Her character became more subdued, her fits of temper more rare. She had long known her

The ruin of the Tuileries, 1871. The shell of the imperial
apartments after their destruction by the Communards.

Paris, 1870. Wounded soldiers from the ramparts arrive at
the quai de la Mégisserie. From a contemporary sketch.

'She wore a little diadem of silver lace': Sarah Bernhardt
as the Queen of Spain in *Ruy Blas*, by Victor Hugo.

own importance, the importance of the theatre; now she learned the pettiness of personal existence, even of personal triumph.

Sarah Bernhardt was awarded a gold medal for her work during the siege. And then the wretched peace was signed. 'A terrible sadness took possession of everyone, even of the people who most ardently longed for peace. Every Parisian felt on his cheek the hand of the victor.' Then came the Commune, and the hideous repression of the Commune. And then, at last, while Paris still breathed in the acrid smell of destruction, the theatres began to re-open. One morning Sarah received a rehearsal notice from the Odéon.

She was soon to have her initiation into the world of greatness. She was cast as the Queen of Spain in the revival of Victor Hugo's *Ruy Blas*. She made Hugo's acquaintance and she was soon his devoted admirer. When he arrived for rehearsals it seemed as if the theatre were illumined.

Ruy Blas was revived on 26 January 1872. Francisque Sarcey, theatre critic for *Le Journal des Débats*, was in ecstasies:

Mlle Sarah Bernhardt has received from nature the gift of melancholy, plaintive dignity. All her movements are noble and harmonious; the long folds of her shot-silver robe arrange themselves about her with poetic grace. Her voice is languishing and tender, her diction so rhythmical, so exquisitely clear that one never loses a syllable even when the words are breathed forth as a caress.

And Théodore de Banville simply wrote: 'Always, until the end of time, men will recall the image of Sarah Bernhardt when Ruy Blas says, "She wore a little diadem of silver lace."' Sarah remembered how, after the performance, the crowds of admirers suddenly made way, and Hugo himself came towards her. 'Before I could say anything, he had knelt down, and, raising my hands to his lips, he murmured: "Thank you, thank you." He was so fine, that evening, with his noble forehead which caught the light, his stubble of silver hair like a crop cut in moonlight, his laughing, shining eyes....'

How far, one wonders, did enchantment lead them? Some say that Sarah was among his mistresses, but it is unlikely that there was a long liaison. Sarah herself, in later life, was to regret that she had not seen more of Victor Hugo. 'I was stupid enough to prefer the company of a bunch of elegant fools to that of the superior men around me.' So she lamented to the composer Reynaldo Hahn. 'Just think of it! One day

I left Victor Hugo in the middle of a conversation and went back to some men from the Jockey Club!' But Victor Hugo was not rejected for a few men-about-town. He had a much more dangerous rival. In 1872 Sarah was enamoured of Jean Mounet-Sully, a young actor who was made, it seems, to play Romantic heroes, to be Hamlet or Orestes, 'and to feel the moving plumes of Achilles shaking upon his brow'. Mounet-Sully was thirty-one, dark, bearded, endowed with pensive eyes and the gift of speaking poetry as if poetry had been his native tongue. Victor Hugo was seventy, and he looked like an old carpenter. For all his gallantry, for all his towering celebrity, he could not match him.

Victor Hugo and his son Charles.
From a photograph taken in Guernsey in 1865.

Jean Mounet-Sully, 'who was made, it seems, to represent the heroes pursued by fate'.
The famous tragic actor (1841–1916) played Hernani to Sarah's Doña Sol, Ruy Blas
to her Queen of Spain, and Hippolyte to her Phèdre. This photograph shows him as
Hamlet in 1893.

A few days after Sarah's dazzling performance in *Ruy Blas*, there came a familiar envelope bearing the circular stamp of the Comédie-Française. The letter was from Émile Perrin, the Administrator-General. He asked to see her.

Duquesnel urged Sarah to stay at the Odéon. He warned her that she still had a year of contract to run, and he refused to increase her salary. Sarah ignored his warning, hurried to the Théâtre-Français, and entered Perrin's office with the words: 'I have come to sign.'

She returned to the stage of the Comédie-Française on 6 November 1872. She took the title-part in Dumas' *Mademoiselle de Belle-Isle*. War and civil war and her own peregrinations from theatre to theatre had made her almost a stranger in the rue de Richelieu. Théodore de Banville, the poet and critic, watching her this November evening, introduced her to his readers as someone almost unknown, described her with a miniaturist's care. We may, for a moment, look at Sarah Bernhardt through his wise and enamoured eyes.

She has one of those delicate, expressive heads that the illuminators of the Middle Ages painted in the miniatures of their manuscripts. Deep, shining, liquid eyes, a straight, fine nose, red lips that open like a flower, revealing the sharp whiteness of the teeth, a long and flexible neck; and all receive unheard-of brilliance from that rich, transparent colouring.... To these strange charms, Mlle Sarah Bernhardt adds one that is still more strange, for her brow is crowned with a heavy, enormous, abundant head of hair, very like the unruly tresses of goddesses, those confusions of light and gold that the sculptors of the Renaissance accumulate on the brows of their Dianas with wild prodigality....

The character of the actress is no less curious than that of the woman. It was from Provost that she learnt pure, elegant and infinitely accurate speech, but nature endowed her with a gift that was rare and strange in quite another way. She was so endowed that whatever she might do she was absolutely and unconsciously lyrical. Her voice, like that of a lyre, holds the rhythm and music of poetry. . . . She receives all her inspiration and all her strength from poetry, and the higher the poetry rises, the more lyrical it grows, the loftier she becomes, the more she is herself....

Make no mistake, the engagement of Mlle Bernhardt at the Comédie-Française is serious and violently revolutionary. It is poetry entering the house of dramatic art; it is the wolf in the fold.

It was at about this time that Sarah began to rehearse the part of Berthe de Savigny in Octave Feuillet's play *Le Sphinx*; and in Feuillet she found yet another bewildered admirer. 'A strange girl,' he wrote

The author of *Le Sphinx*: Octave Feuillet,
the popular novelist and playwright (1821–90).

home to his wife. 'It's the first time in my long career that I've met the real actress of the novels, the courtesan-actress of the eighteenth century.' When Mme Feuillet attended the last rehearsals she, too, was spellbound by Berthe de Savigny. 'Thin and diaphanous, she seemed to struggle to drag her impalpable body along. . . . She seemed at times like a wandering shadow. . . . This Sarah, of so fatal but so delicate a beauty, had extraordinary dramatic powers. She had unexpected feelings, too, and proved most touching in the fourth act, as the sacrificed woman. This part of the play was a real triumph for her at the first performance.'

Sarah established herself at once in the rue de Richelieu, and began to dabble in power politics; indeed, there was constant conflict between the new *pensionnaire* and M. l'administrateur-général de la Comédie-Française. Since Perrin did not give her enough work to satisfy her, she determined to become a sculptor. Wholehearted as ever, she rented a studio near the place Clichy, where friends and lovers came to admire, take counsel, and, at five o'clock, take tea. There were – it was said – three famous times in Paris: one o'clock, Gambetta smoked his second cigar. Four o'clock, prices fell at the Bourse. Five o'clock, Sarah received for tea.

But her sculpture was more than a social pastime. The following year she sent her first exhibit to the Salon: a marble bust of her sister Régina; and if the jury accepted it out of consideration for her fame, if they dismissed her sculpture as a transient caprice, they were mistaken. Sarah set to work with characteristic ferocity. 'I did not have a clock, or a watch with me,' she wrote in her memoirs. 'I wanted not to know the time, except when I was performing; and then a maid used to come in search of me. How often I went without *déjeuner* and dinner, because I had forgotten! And then I was reminded because I fainted from exhaustion, and I quickly sent someone out for cakes.' She took lessons in sculpture from Matthieu Meusnier, and in 1876 the Salon catalogue recorded a plaster group, *Après la Tempête*, and a bronze bust. The sculptor received an honourable mention. She earned not only a *succès d'estime* but, it seems, a *succès d'argent*. In time she sculpted a bust of herself which (so legend said) she sold for 20,000 francs to the Grand Duke Constantine of Russia.

At every Exhibition [wrote an admiring critic in 1879] she arrives with something new; here is the bust of Émile de Girardin; there is the bust of

Between the acts. Sarah Bernhardt in her dressing-room. The negro page also kept guard outside her suite when she stayed at the Savoy Hotel in London. This picture comes from *Le Figaro illustré*, 1894.

A SARAH BERNHARDT

JULES BASTIEN=LEPAGE. 1879

Busnach, the vaudeville-writer. This year she is exhibiting the busts of her friend Mlle Abbéma and Miss X....

Sarah Bernhardt is not content with modelling, she wants to paint. Nothing deters this woman, artistic *par excellence*; after a lesson or two she catches a most remarkable likeness; and France has an artist the more. Everyone has seen her self-portrait, exhibited at the *Nouveau Journal*. . . .

And when it is no longer enough for Sarah to be an exhibitor, when she wants to turn critic, the fairy who has been with her since birth simply raises a hand; *Le Globe* is founded, and Doña Sol is promptly asked if she will do the Salon.

Look at this young woman with her red-tinted, slightly dishevelled hair. She has been rehearsing at the Comédie-Française. She collapses into the carriage murmuring: 'I'm exhausted!'

It is She. The driver cracks his whip and the horses canter off towards the Palais de l'Industrie. And there she does a steeplechase round the galleries, stopping a minute in front of every picture; with the calm and assurance of Napoleon she dictates her decrees to three or four young and devoted secretaries, who absorb her words and inscribe them, respectfully, in a notebook, then and there. She hasn't time to write, she thinks aloud, and after her talk and walk the copy's done, the paper prints it in all its vivacity and circulates it among the avid readers, who *must know* what Sarah thinks of this or that picture.

Sarah the artist and sculptor demanded Sarah the anatomist; and the students of l'École pratique de médecine soon observed Sarah Bernhardt, escorted by a doctor, pursuing her studies in the dissecting-room, prodding corpses with her parasol.

Small wonder that truth and rumour spread unceasingly; that Sarah became the constant sphinx of Paris; that Sarah's private life became a favourite topic in print and conversation. Small wonder that Clément Clament, in his book on Sarah, wrote vividly of her *hôtel*, 4, rue de Rome, where

stuffed vultures, holding skulls in their claws, have long been the ornament of her salon, in company with a leering skeleton. The masters of the house were a young monkey, very ill brought-up, and a litter of dogs and cats reared by hand by their mistress, who would not entrust the task to anyone.

In her bedroom is the famous coffin, quilted in pink; another kind of fantasy, this little piece of furniture, though it will never, in any country, be considered as a *love-nest*.

Never? Marie Colombier thought otherwise when she published her scurrilous *Mémoires de Sarah Barnum*. Sarah, she wrote, 'demanded that

Sarah Bernhardt in 1879, the year of her first visit to London.
From the portrait by Jules Bastien-Lepage.

ABOVE Sarah Bernhardt, artist. From a photograph taken in her studio, 1878–9, while she was working on her Palm Sunday picture. This painting, she recorded, was bought by Prince Leopold, son of Queen Victoria.

OPPOSITE Sarah Bernhardt, sculptor. From a photograph by Melandri.

her intimate friends should keep her company in the narrow box. Some of them hesitated, because this funereal furniture killed their desires.'

'I have been one of the great lovers of my century,' said Sarah once to her close friend Suze Rueff. Her lovers were of course a topic of perennial interest and constant innuendo; and Clament eagerly repeated the tale of Sarah, anaesthetized for some minor operation, 'chattering, nattering, talking of Peter and Paul, revealing facts and creating vivid fictions, while the doctor administered chloroform with a vengeance to save his face'.

And Sarah's menagerie was a topic hardly less fruitful: a theme for the wildest journalistic fantasia.

Mlle Sarah Bernhardt [reported a journalist, with his tongue in his cheek] has sanguinary tastes, ferocious instincts, and knowing that you cannot cut up human beings with impunity, she makes up for it with animals.

You cannot conceive the horrible pastimes thought up by this young and charming woman, in appearance so gentle and so frail....

The other day she found herself with a few friends in her studio. Growing impatient with the gambols of a kitten, she caught hold of the little animal by the skin of its neck and threw it alive into a stove of burning coal....

Mlle Sarah Bernhardt, so people say, has with her own white hands poisoned two monkeys that have ceased to please her.

She has cut off a dog's head to try and solve the problem of life after decapitation.

Some people, more audaciously, have ventured to insinuate that the famous skeleton Lazarus, which Mlle Bernhardt keeps in her bedroom, might well be another victim of the terrible actress....

And the police? They know about it, so people say, but they can do nothing. We are short of actresses; when we are fortunate enough to find one, it is better to shut our eyes to the weaknesses of her private life.

One day [so Sarah remembered], Perrin came to see me in my sculptor's studio. He began by chatting about my busts, and said I should do a medallion of him; and then, as if by chance, he asked if I knew the part of Phèdre. Until then I had only played the part of Aricie, and the part of Phèdre seemed formidable. None the less, I had studied it for pleasure. 'Yes, I know the part. But I think that if I had to perform it, I should die of fright.'

He laughed, his little nasal laugh, and said as he kissed my hand (for he was very gallant): 'Work on it, I think that you will play it.'

And indeed, a week later, I was summoned to the director's office, and Perrin told me that he was announcing *Phèdre* for 21 December, Racine's birthday, with Mlle Sarah Bernhardt in the title-rôle.

56

Phèdre was the most demanding, most prestigious part in all French drama. Phèdre was the reef on which all but the greatest of actresses must founder; and though it was certain that Sarah would bring her poetic feeling, her magic diction, her sculptural, classic gestures to the part, it was felt that sometimes her physical strength might fail her.

This was indeed what happened; in the fourth act, in the terrible scene when Phèdre learned that Hippolyte loved Aricie, Sarah visibly weakened, her voice betrayed her, and she struggled to express the passions that she knew so well. The mantle of Phèdre was too heavy for her delicate frame. But in the scenes that exacted less evident strength, she was excellent, and some thought that the famous declaration had never been recited with more contained passion, with finer consciousness of the shades of meaning.

Sarah herself was convinced that Rachel's Phèdre was unique, could not have been surpassed; and this although she had never seen Rachel on the stage. But if Rachel recalled the statues of ancient Greece, Sarah conjured before the eyes of the audience the living woman of antiquity, and she had no need to study her sobs. Her tears were always close to the surface, and they flowed easily, with heart-breaking realism. Sarah would always abandon herself to Phèdre as she abandoned herself to no other part. Perhaps her supreme achievement was her Phèdre. When she played Phèdre she always needed to prepare herself with a long interval of quiet reflection. But, as Maurice Baring was to write, from the moment she staggered on to the stage, trembling under the load of her unconfessed passion, 'the spectator witnessed the building up of a miraculous piece of architecture in time and space, and followed the progression, the rise, the crisis, and the tranquil close of a mysterious symphony.'

It was in the New Year, 1875, soon after her first performance in *Phèdre*, that Sarah was made a *sociétaire* of the Comédie-Française.

The honour did not wholly please her.

From that moment [so she wrote], I felt as if I were in prison, as if I had agreed to stay at the Maison de Molière for many years. The thought of this made me unhappy. It was Perrin who had urged me to demand the *sociétariat*. And now I regretted it.

For the rest of the year I performed only occasionally. I spent all my time supervising the construction of a pretty *hôtel* which I was having built for myself....

Sarah Bernhardt
as Phèdre.
From a photograph
by Downey.

Sarah Bernhardt's *hôtel* in Paris.
From a contemporary engraving.

My dream was to have a home that was really my own; and so I fulfilled it. M. Régnier's son-in-law, Félix Escalier, was a very fashionable architect, and he built me a delightful *hôtel*.

There was nothing I liked better than to go round the scaffolding with him in the mornings.... And then I used to climb up on the roof. I forgot my theatrical troubles in this new occupation. God knows, I even dreamed of turning architect.

Then, when the building was finished, I had to think about the interior. And I spent my energy helping my artist friends to paint the ceilings....

Let us look at the new *hôtel* through the eyes of an English journalist, the author of *Celebrities at Home*.

You would say at once [he wrote] it was the home of an artist. It is in the artists' quarter. They dwell in sky-parlours at Batignolles or in the *pays Latin* while they are learning how to make their fortunes, and in villas bordering the Parc Monceau when they have learned. The streets are named after great workers with the brush, living or dead; one of them for instance, bears the

The author of *La Dame aux camélias*: Alexandre Dumas
fils (1824–95). From a photograph by Nadar.

name of Fortuny; and it is at the corner of this rue Fortuny and the avenue
de Villiers that Sarah Bernhardt lives, in a house lately built from her own
designs. It is half studio, half mansion. The drawing-room window is large
enough to illumine a cathedral, and there is as much skylight as roof. . . . But
is it a drawing-room or is it a studio?. . . It is a very broad, very lofty, lit both
by the cathedral-window aforesaid and by a skylight – in consequence a
studio. It is tapestried in velvet – a drawing-room then. It contains easels,
unfinished pictures, busts in the rough – studio; daintily-fashioned chairs,
fauteuils, satin couches – drawing-room; vases big as sentry-boxes, which may
have come direct from the sale of the furniture and effects of the leader of
the Forty Thieves – drawing-room again, if you like, but a drawing-room of
Brobdingnag. And to add to the variety of effects, towering tropical plants
enough for Kew, and a fireplace worthy, in breadth and depth, of the kitchen
at Windsor Castle.

On 14 February 1876, Sarah appeared as Mistress Clarkson in *L'Étrangère*, the first acknowledged play by Dumas *fils* to be performed at the

The Comédie-Française in their green-room, 1880. Sarah Bernhardt,
in pensive mood, is seated left of centre.

SARAH BERNHARDT

'The divine Sarah': one of the best of the early photographs.

Théâtre-Français. 'I confess', wrote Henry James, 'that *L'Étrangère* strikes me as a rather desperate piece of floundering in the dramatic sea.... The *Foreigner* is played by that very interesting actress, Mme Sarah Bernhardt. . . . [But she] is like the heroine of an old-fashioned drama of the Boulevard du Crime who has strayed unwittingly into a literary work.' Sarcey, like Henry James, considered the play an extraordinary medley. As for the famous speech in which Mrs Clarkson told the story of her life, he considered it 'a tissue of extravagances and useless vulgarities. If Mlle Sarah Bernhardt had not cast the fascinating poetry of her gesture and diction over such romantic idiocies, the public would have burst out laughing.'

It was, indeed, largely Sarah's magic that established the play. When the curtain rose on the third act to show her radiant in her white silk dress, trimmed with lace, upon her couch, she seemed the living image of Mme Récamier; and when she spoke 'she sent a kiss to the public with every word'. A delighted Dumas offered her a copy of *L'Étrangère* 'with the thanks and the unreserved compliments of the author'.

It was a measure of Sarah's powers that her next impressive part was a part she performed that autumn, the part of Posthumia in Alexandre Parodi's *Rome vaincue*. She had, in fact, refused the part of the vestal virgin and demanded that of the blind old woman of seventy.

Even Sarcey, who made and unmade the success of plays, wrote a panegyric about Sarah:

She displayed qualities of energy and pathos that even her admirers did not suspect in her.

She was wonderfully dressed and wonderfully made-up. A wasted, wrinkled face of extraordinary majesty: vague, dull eyes, a cloak which fell at her sides when she raised her arms and seemed like the vast wings of some gigantic, sinister bat. There could be nothing more terrible, more poetic....

It was no longer an actress; it was nature itself, served by a wonderful intelligence, a soul of fire, by the clearest, the most melodious voice that has ever enchanted human ears. This woman acts with her heart, with her whole being. She dares gestures that would in anyone else be ridiculous, and they sweep an audience off its feet....

'As for Mlle Sarah Bernhardt,' added Henry James, as a postcript, 'she is simply, at present, in Paris, one of the great figures of the day. It would be hard to imagine a more brilliant embodiment of feminine success.'

OVERLEAF Sarah Bernhardt as Adrienne Lecouvreur, in her own play of that name. From a photograph taken in 1905 by W. and D. Downey.

For years, now, she had moved among the elect; she had earned the homage of Victor Hugo. She had dined with that most engaging, most misunderstood Romantic, Théophile Gautier. 'There was an oriental nobility about him, stifled by fashion and by western manners. I knew nearly all his poetry,' she remembered, 'and I looked affectionately on that gentle-hearted man in love with beauty. I liked, in imagination, to clothe him in splendid oriental dress. In my mind's eye I saw him lazing on big cushions, plunging his fine hands among jewels of every colour. . . .' And Sarah was also the friend of Émile de Girardin, the founder of the popular Press in France.

Among my friends were a dozen leaders of different opinions, and I was interested in them all: the wildest, and the most wise.

I often saw Gambetta at Girardin's, and it was a delight for me to listen to that wonderful man. His words were so wise, so considered, and so convincing. . . .

Besides, Gambetta was never banal, never ordinary. . . .

When he was tired of politics, he used to talk literature, and he was peculiarly charming; he knew everything, and he recited poetry to admiration.

One evening, after a dinner at Girardin's, he and I performed the whole scene with Doña Sol from the first act of *Hernani*. And, if he was not as handsome as Mounet-Sully, he was quite as wonderful. . . .

It was *Hernani* which finally established Sarah with the public, the triumphant *Hernani* of 21 November 1877. Mounet-Sully, in all his beauty, all the splendour of his talent, played Hernani to Sarah's Doña Sol. And after the performance Hugo wrote to her: 'Madame, you were great and charming; you moved me, the old warrior himself; and, at a certain moment, while a touched, enchanted public applauded you, I wept. The tear that you inspired is yours, and I lay it at your feet.' With the letter came a gold bracelet with a diamond pendant. Sarah later lost the diamond at Alfred Sassoon's, but she would not let him replace it. No Sassoon could return her Victor Hugo's tear.

Sarah was not only, now, the darling of the public; she was the darling of the critics, too. Her colleagues at the Comédie were, understandably, a little jealous, and Perrin – so she tells us – was constantly picking quarrels with her. It offended his sense of self-importance that she should not depend on him; and, as he always refused her requests, she now simply sent them over his head to M. le Ministre des Beaux-Arts, and they were promptly granted. During the Paris Exhibition of 1878 Perrin was given yet more cause for exasperation. In the *Doña Sol*, an

Sarah Bernhardt as Doña Sol in *Hernani*, by Victor Hugo.

orange balloon made specially for the occasion, she made an ascent from the exhibition site.

In a fantasy, published that year, *Dans les Nuages: Impressions d'une Chaise*, Sarah even described her flight as it might have appeared to the chair she used on her ascent. Rapidly they rose from the crowded exhibition, 'and then nothing! Nothing! ... The earth below, the sky above... I'm in the clouds, I've left Paris in the mist, I find a blue sky and a radiant sun. The little basket plunges into a milky vapour all warm with sunshine. Round us are opaque mountains with iridescent crests.... It's wonderful! Stupefying!' Over the Pont de la Concorde they drifted, over the Tuileries, where the crowd in the courtyard rushed towards the *quais* to follow the escapade. The balloon drifted on, over Père-Lachaise, and Sarah stripped the petals off her corsage and scattered them over the cemetery. At half past six she began to make foie-gras sandwiches; they uncorked a bottle of champagne and drank to the future of ballooning, to glory, to the arts, to what has been, is, and will be, and tossed the empty bottle into the Lac de Vincennes. Long after nightfall they landed at Verchère and returned to an apprehensive avenue de Villiers.

Perrin, that model of officialdom, fined Sarah 1000 francs for making a journey without leave. Sarah retorted that she would not pay, and that she would resign from the Comédie-Française. Once again M. le Ministre des Beaux-Arts intervened; he declared that Perrin had exceeded his rights, that the fine was cancelled, and that Sarah should withdraw her resignation. Triumphantly she did so.

... But [so she wrote in her memoirs] the situation was tense. My celebrity had become enervating for my enemies, and a little clamorous even for my friends. As for me, at that time, I found the commotion vastly entertaining. I did nothing to attract attention. My somewhat fantastic tastes, my thinness, my pallor, my very personal style of dress, my scorn of fashion, my disregard of everything, made me into someone apart.

I had no idea of it. I did not read the papers (I've never read them). And so I was unaware of everything, good or bad, that was said about me. Surrounded by a court of worshippers, I lived on in my sunlit dream. All the royalty, all the celebrities who were the guests of France during the Exhibition came to call on me. The procession much amused me.

When, in the first weeks of 1879, the unfortunate M. Perrin decided to revive *Mithridate*, he was thinking especially of Monime, and hoping that – at least among the elect – Sarah would have a brilliant success. But Sarah took small interest in the theatre. 'I shouldn't mind a *sociétaire* who sculpted in her free time,' said the despondent Perrin to Sarcey. 'What I cannot accept, what distresses me, is that I have a sculptor who dabbles in the theatre if she has a moment to spare.'

One day, when Sarah was unwell, Perrin came to see her.

He gave me a lecture [she recalled]. 'You're killing yourself, my dear child, why are you doing sculpture? Painting? Is it to prove to yourself that you can do it?' 'No, no, it isn't!' I cried. 'I have to make it necessary to stay here.' 'I don't understand...,' said Perrin. He was very attentive.

'Well, I have a wild longing to travel, to see something else, to breathe another air, to see skies which are not so low as ours. I want to see bigger trees, I want just to see something different! And I'm creating tasks for myself to keep myself on the chain. If I didn't, I think that my longing to know and to see would win the day, and I should do something silly!'

And so the sculpture continued. It is said that when, this year, Charles Garnier – the architect of the Paris Opéra – designed the theatre in Monte Carlo, Sarah was not content to recite a prologue at the opening, but sent off one of her statues for the façade (Gustave Doré was asked to make the other). Garnier found her statue of Music inadequate, and put it – with Doré's offering – in the vaults of the theatre. Sarah was more successful as a critic. It was this spring that Flaubert, advising his artist niece to cultivate the critics, offered to call on Sarah Bernhardt, critic of *Le Globe*.

It was now, on 2 April 1879, at the apogee of her career, that Sarah first played opposite Mounet-Sully the part of the Queen in *Ruy Blas*.

She came on stage, as so often, stricken with fear, trembling so much that she could only indicate some of her gestures. But 'Sarah Bernhardt, always so pretty, so elegant, so artistic, has never perhaps been so adorably dressed,' wrote Arnold Mortier in *Les Soirées parisiennes*. 'It was poetry in costume. Nor has a real queen ever been more queenly than this queen of the theatre in her magnificent dress in the second act: a white satin dress with silver embroideries, a train in figured silk; a little crown on top of her hair.' And it was not only her appearance that enchanted the house. As she played that night opposite Mounet-Sully, she had, wrote Sarcey, 'all the tender, languorous grace of the part. There are words that she said to perfection, with exquisite delicacy; others she hurled away with the impulse of a passion breaking

71

its banks.' Hugo's most lyrical passages seemed, as Sarah spoke them, like a long caress. 'She only added the music of her voice to the music of the verse.'

Flowers filled her dressing-room, the corridor was heaped with roses, violets and lilac. And years later, inscribing a book to her, Victor Hugo could only inscribe it 'to the Queen whose Ruy Blas I should have wished to be.' Perrin, too, was glad that Sarah drew such multitudes to the theatre; but he would have been even more pleased (so she considered) if the applause had been accorded to another. The more that Sarah triumphed, the more he understood his own ineffectiveness. Her independence drove him to silent fury.

It was evident that the tension could not last, that sooner rather than later there would be a dramatic change. It came with the arrival of William Jarrett.

One day [recalled Sarah] my servant came to tell me that an elderly English-man was asking to see me with such insistence that, in spite of my orders, he thought he should come and inform me. 'Send the man away, and let me work.' I had just begun a picture which absorbed me: a young girl, holding an armful of palms, on Palm Sunday. The little Italian model who was posing was an entrancing child of eight years old. Suddenly she said to me: 'Arguing, the Englishman . . .'

And indeed I heard the sound of increasing argument in the next room. I went out, palette in hand, determined to send the intruder away; but, just as I opened my studio door, a tall man came forward, so close to me that I had to step back; and he therefore came into my hall. He had bright, hard eyes, silver hair, a well-kept beard; he apologized, very correctly, for disturb-ing me, he admired my painting, my sculpture, my hall: so much so that I still didn't know his name.

After ten minutes, I asked him to sit down and tell me the purpose of his visit. He began quietly, and with a marked accent: 'I am Mr Jarrett, impre-sario. Do you want to come to America?' 'Never in my life!' I cried, fiercely. 'Never! Never!' 'All right. Never mind. Here is my address. Don't lose it.'

As Jarrett left the room he mentioned that there would be a further fortune to earn if she gave private performances in London. Sarah had met her match, and signed the contract. Jarrett inspired her with con-fidence from the first; and that confidence, so she wrote some thirty years later, was never lost.

Perrin and the committee of the Comédie-Française had in fact arranged for a French season in London; they had signed a contract with John Hollingshead, manager of the Gaiety Theatre. No one had been consulted on the decision, and Sarah understandably disapproved of such high-handed behaviour. Her tacit but very evident disapproval caused Perrin anxiety, and he asked her what she contemplated. Sarah demanded to be made an independent *sociétaire* for the length of the London season.

This agreeable status would allow her to give as many private performances as she wanted. But she made this demand of a Comédie already exasperated by her behaviour; and the committee refused it. Sarah might not have crossed the Channel in this sultry, significant summer if John Hollingshead had not made his pronouncement. He simply said that if Sarah, Croizette, Coquelin or Mounet-Sully failed to appear in London, the contract would be annulled.

Sarah was for once alarmed at the damage she might cause the Comédie. She called on Perrin, and declared she was ready to go to London on any terms. The committee promptly created both Sarah and Croizette independent *sociétaires* in perpetuity. Perrin and Sarah embraced each other, peace was once more restored, and final preparations began.

This bronze medallion was struck in Prague in honour of Sarah Bernhardt and Alphonse Mucha. Round the edge are listed those rôles of Sarah's for which Mucha produced posters.

3
Sarah
the Conqueror

'She will always be one of the permanent and beautiful guesses
of mankind.' So wrote Maurice Baring. This early photograph of
Sarah Bernhardt suggests a little of her mystery.

IT WAS ON A MAY MORNING in 1879, the day before the Whitsun holiday, that Sarah Bernhardt landed at Folkestone. '*Vive* Sarah Bernhardt!' cried a young man who looked like Hamlet and handed her a gardenia. It was Forbes Robertson. 'They will soon be making you a carpet of flowers,' said a jealous colleague. 'Here it is!' cried another worshipper, casting an armful of lilies at her feet. This was Oscar Wilde; and Wilde led the cheers as the Comédie-Française boarded the train for London.

From that moment, Sarah Bernhardt was the cynosure of every eye, and the favourite theme of every conversation. And at 77 Chester Square, where she was to live during her stay, the door stood open, the lights inside invited her to enter, and an enormous, radiant bouquet was waiting, with a card inscribed: 'Welcome! Henry Irving.'

Next day was devoted to receiving the Press. Thirty-seven journalists came, and Jarrett spared her none of them. 'That man,' she wrote, admiringly, 'had a genius for publicity.... He had imposed himself upon me by his intelligence, his sense of humour, and by my need to be guided in this country which was new to me. "No," he said to me, "if you receive them all together, they will be furious, and you will have a bad Press. You must receive them one after the other."' Sarah duly received them all; but, as she spoke no English, it was Jarrett who spoke to them, translating or inventing her comments for her.

The thirty-seven journalists had hardly left Chester Square before a duchess arrived to pay a call. Sarah's social life had begun. And, from the first, Sarah delighted in it. She went to her first dinner-party in London, at a peeress's house in Prince's Gate. 'There were some twenty people there.... I had been told that the food was very bad in England; I found the dinner perfect. I had been told that the English were cold and formal; I found them charming, and full of humour. Everyone spoke French very well. I was ashamed of my ignorance of English.... I came home very happy and very much an anglomaniac.'

Next day, a sparkling summer day, she went to Rotten Row.

The whole of Hyde Park seemed to be strewn with enormous bouquets. This was not only because of the clumps of trees, wonderfully arranged by the gardeners. It was also because of the clusters of parasols: blue and pink, red, yellow and white, which shaded bright hats covered with flowers; and beneath these hats shone the pretty faces of women and babies.

Along the riding track itself, there was a dizzy gallop of elegant thoroughbreds bearing hundreds of women riders, keen and lithe and bold. Then there

77

Sarah Bernhardt. From a photograph taken in 1884.

were men riders and children on big Irish ponies, and other children galloping on Shetland ponies with long, thick manes. And the children's hair, the horses' manes, were blowing with the speed of the ride.

The carriage drive, which lay between the riders and the pedestrians, was streaked with dog-carts, barouches, mail-coaches [*sic*], eight-spring carriages, and extremely elegant cabs; powdered valets, decked-out horses, sporting drivers, ladies boldly managing wonderful trotters.

All this elegance, all this perfume of luxury, all this zest for living conjured up the memory of our Bois de Boulogne. It was so elegant and so alive, a few years earlier, when Napoleon III used to pass through it in his postilion-carriage, nonchalant and smiling. Oh, how pretty it was, our Bois de Boulogne!...

I closed my eyes in anguish at the fearful memory of 1870....

Then I opened my eyes once more, and, through the mist of tears, I caught another glimpse of the triumphant vitality around me.

On 2 June 1879, at the Gaiety Theatre, the Comédie-Française were to open their London season with *Le Misanthrope*, the second act of *Phèdre*, and *Les Précieuses ridicules*. At a quarter past ten that night Sarah Bernhardt was due to give her first performance to an English audience. She brought her own enveloping aura of legends, passions and eccentricities, her own theatrical reputation. Far more dangerous, far more exacting, she also brought with her the aura and the legend of Rachel. It was twenty-four years since Rachel had last taken London by storm, and there must have been many in the audience who remembered her, many who instinctively compared. It was typical of Sarah that she began deliberately, defiantly, with the part that had been Rachel's most lasting triumph.

In her dressing-room at the Gaiety, stage-fright overcame her.

Three times I put rouge on my cheeks and shadow on my eyes; three times I took it all off with a sponge. I thought I was ugly. I thought I was thinner. I thought I was shorter.

I shut my eyes, to listen to my voice.... My voice was husky in the low notes, clouded in the soprano notes. I wept with rage.

They came to say that the second act of *Phèdre* was about to begin. I went mad. I didn't have my veil. I didn't have my rings. My belt of cameos was not fastened. I murmured:

> *Le voici. Vers mon cœur tout mon sang se retire ...*
>
> *J'oublie, en le voyant ...*

I was struck by the word '*j'oublie* – I forget.' Suppose I were to forget what I had to say!

78

And in fact ... what was I saying? I didn't know any more.... What did I say after '*en le voyant*'? No-one answered. I terrified them all by my state of nerves. I heard Got murmur: 'She's going mad!' Mlle Thénard, who was playing Œnone, my old nurse, said to me: 'Don't worry, all the English have gone to Paris, there are only Belgians in the audience!'

This wildly comical reply sent my mind off on another tack. 'You're silly!' I said. 'You know quite well how frightened I was in Brussels.' 'Oh, that was quite unnecessary,' Mlle Thénard answered, coldly. 'There were only English there that day.'

I had to go on stage. I had no time to answer her; but she had changed the course of my ideas.

I had stage-fright. Not the kind that paralyses, but the kind that sends you mad. It is quite enough, but it's better. You do too much, but at least you do something.

The whole audience applauded for several seconds when I went on stage; and, as I bowed in acknowledgment, I said inside myself: 'Yes, yes ... you'll see ... I'm going to give you my blood, ... my life, ... my soul ...' ...

I suffered, I wept, I implored, I cried; and all of it was real; my suffering was horrible, the tears that flowed were burning and bitter. I implored Hippolyte for the love that was killing me, and the arms that I stretched out to Mounet-Sully were the arms of Phèdre, tense with the cruel longing to embrace. The god had come.

She had met London across the footlights – and she had roused it to fever pitch. Few audiences in her career were to be so impassioned. 'We remember Rachel's sombre grandeur,' said *The Times*, 'the concentrated passion that seemed to be glowing at a red heat in the core of her heart. Her Phèdre might be more terrible and intense, but it was, perhaps, less womanlike, less sympathetic, less *entraînante* than the Phèdre of Sarah Bernhardt.... 'When she advanced alone to the footlights,' wrote another spectator, 'in the speech in which she acknowledges and laments her unhappy love – there was deep silence. No one could clap; we could only pant and clench our hands. The slow, emphatic declamation, the small white muscular face, were too impressive – the tragedy appeared too awful a reality.'

Sarah's determination to conquer London, the perpetual passion of her performance, had exhausted her. That night she was shaken by a fit of coughing. Dr Parrot, who had long attended her, was summoned to London. He arrived next afternoon and forbade her to perform that evening. Parrot's orders decided her. She asked him to leave the room, dressed herself rapidly, and sped off in a hansom to the theatre. Parrot

79

went the way of all who failed to comply with Sarah's wishes. Half an hour later her maid brought a letter from him, full of affection and fury, reproaches and advice. He also enclosed a prescription in case of relapse. He was returning to Paris within the hour.

Parrot's reproaches were deserved. Three times Sarah fainted as she dressed for *L'Étrangère*. When at last she came on stage she was dulled with opium and she walked as if she were in a dream. The first act was irreproachable; but in the third, when she was about to tell the Duchesse de Septmonts the story of her life, Mrs Clarkson lost her memory. In vain the Duchesse prompted her, mimed the words, made signs. Mrs Clarkson could not lip-read, could not even hear. And then, at last, she said: 'Madame, I asked you here to tell you why I have behaved like this.... I've thought it over, I'm not going to tell you to-day.'

Sophie Croizette, Duchesse de Septmonts, looked at her aghast, then rose and walked off stage. Constant Coquelin, Duc de Septmonts, was rushed in to bring the act to an end. Sarah had cut the great scene of *L'Étrangère*; and she remained blissfully unaware that she had done something unusual.

However strangely Sarah performed that night, the audience had no eyes for anyone else. Even Francisque Sarcey – who had bustled across the Channel – found that he was basking in her glory. 'Nothing,' he wrote back to Paris, 'nothing can give an idea of the craze that Mlle Sarah Bernhardt is exciting. It's a mania.'

When the Lamia-like Mrs Clarkson became the virginal, adoring Doña Sol, Victorian London was entranced. It was, indeed, a Pre-Raphaelite performance. 'And all this, when it finds speech, translated into the soft music of the sweetest voice we have ever heard upon the stage.... In Doña Sol she is all the part permits her to be.'

In all this chorus of praise there was one dissentient voice; but it was the voice of Matthew Arnold, and perhaps it made the most illuminating comment.

One talks vaguely of genius [he wrote], but I had never till now comprehended how much of Rachel's superiority was purely in intellectual power, how eminently this power counts in the actor's art as in all art.... Temperament and quick intelligence, passion, nervous mobility, grace, smile, voice, charm, poetry, – Mlle Sarah Bernhardt has them all. One watches her with pleasure, with admiration, – and yet not without a secret disquietude. Something is wanting, or, at least, not present in sufficient force; something which alone can secure and fix her administration of all the charming gifts which she has, can alone keep them fresh, keep them sincere, save them from perils by caprice, perils by mannerism. That something is high intellectual power. It was here that Rachel was so great; she began, one says to oneself as one recalls her image and dwells upon it, – she began almost where Mlle Sarah Bernhardt ends.

Sarah's personal triumph in 1879 equalled that of Rachel in that London season of thirty-nine years before; but perhaps, this time, the triumph owed something to intense publicity. Sarah was not, like Rachel, exclusively given to her art; there was far more of the Barnum about her, far more of the *cabotine*, and publicity methods had progressed in the last few decades. However, the Press was full of her doings; and not only did the critics rave, but *Punch* addressed a poem to her, and celebrated her triumphs in 'The Divine Sarah' – a cartoon by Du Maurier. Two elegant young men were talking together in a club.

FIRST CRITIC (aetat 21): 'Beats Rachel hollow in Ong-dromack, hanged if she don't!'

SECOND CRITIC (ditto): 'So I think, old man! And in L'Étronjair she licks Mademoiselle Mars all to fits!'

Whatever the reasons for Sarah's triumph, every seat in the Gaiety was booked, now, for her Phèdre. The guinea stall on Sarah's nights was, we are told, 'often sold by *abonnés* for five times the amount'. Sarah was also enjoying a constant social triumph.

> *Chester Square, habiteras.*
> *À Rotten Row, tu monteras.*
> *Le Parlement, visiteras.*
> *Garden-parties, fréquenteras.*
> *Chaque visite, tu rendras.*
> *À chaque lettre, répondras.*
> *Photographies, tu signeras. . . .*

So went the social commandments sent out from Paris. But Sarah had no time for the code. She was exquisite, but she was exasperating. She received hundreds of letters which she never answered. She accepted invitations and failed to appear, or disturbed all arrangements by preposterous unpunctuality. One of her first engagements, so we are told, was at the house of the octogenarian Lady Combermere. A roomful of guests, packed in several ranks of gold chairs, awaited her for an hour. At last there was the sound of an arrival. Sarah was slowly and nonchalantly mounting the staircase, when from the landing her manager 'hurled an opprobrious epithet at her'.

Sir Algernon Borthwick of *The Morning Post* (later Lord Glenesk) was more fortunate than Lady Combermere. He not only persuaded Sarah to give a private performance in Eaton Place, but even received a bronze inkstand modelled by herself and representing her head on the body of a sphinx. For years the 'letters of friendship and gossip' were to speed to and fro between them; and it was at a Borthwick breakfast that Sarah first met Lily Langtry, who recorded her impressions of the French actress.

This great and overwhelming artist was almost too individual, too exotic, to be completely understood or properly estimated *all at once*. Her superb diction, her lovely silken voice, her natural acting, her passionate temperament, her fire – in a word, transcendent genius – caused amazement. . . . She filled the imagination as a great poet might do. . . .

She gowned herself beautifully, wearing mostly long, trailing white garments, richly embroidered and beaded, as was the fashion of the time. Around her throat she tied the large bow of tulle made familiar in Georges Clairin's painting. . . .

Painters and poets admired her. Oscar Wilde enthused over her likeness to coins of the ancient Romans, and carried me off to the British Museum to hunt for her profile in coins, intaglios, and vases of the period. . . .

While Mrs Langtry was tripping round the British Museum, Sarah herself appeared in *Andromaque*, and held an exhibition of her sculpture and painting in a gallery in Piccadilly. A hundred invitations had been sent out, and, much to her delight, twelve hundred guests arrived. The Prince and Princess of Wales had promised to attend, and

M. Gladstone [Sarah recorded] did me the great honour of talking to me for more than ten minutes. This man, with his original mind, talked about everything with a quite remarkable grace. He asked me what I felt about the attacks which certain preachers were launching against the Comédie-Française – and against the damnable acting profession.

I answered that I found our art as profitable to morality as the sermon of a Protestant or Catholic priest.

'But, Mademoiselle, tell me what moral lesson we should draw from *Phèdre*?'

'Oh, Monsieur Gladstone, you rather surprise me. *Phèdre* is a classical tragedy, so the customs and morality cannot be seen in the same way as our own,

Two of Sarah Bernhardt's admirers: the Prince and Princess of Wales,
later King Edward VII and Queen Alexandra.

or as the morality of today.... The love of Phèdre is excused by the fatality which weighs upon her family, and descends upon her without pity.... As for Thésée, his verdict without appeal, his monstrous and arbitrary act, is punished by the death of this greatly loved son, the last and only hope of his life. One should never do anything irreparable!'

'Ah!' the great man answered gravely, 'so you are against the death penalty?'

'Yes, Monsieur Gladstone.'

'You are right, Mademoiselle.'

Frederic Leighton came to join us, and he was kind enough to compliment me on my picture of a young girl bearing palms. This picture was bought by Prince Leopold.

It was a happy artist who spent her earnings on a cheetah and a wolfhound. Alas, the staff at Chester Square did not share her pleasure; and when the cheetah was freed in the garden and set upon Sarah's four dogs, and Bizibouzou the parrot screamed stridently, and Darwin the monkey ground his teeth and rocked his cage, every window in Chester Square flew open. Victorian London watched with amusement, amazement and dismay.

Sarah's immense popularity raised a storm of jealousy within the Comédie; and a swarm of malevolent rumours were soon buzzing in the Press. It was said that for an admission fee of a shilling one could see Sarah Bernhardt in male dress; that she might be observed, free of charge, on her balcony, smoking giant cigars; that she dressed in pierrot's clothes, and took boxing lessons. It seemed that the English public began to believe the *canards* of the French Press, for an English tailor offered to make a man's suit for her free of charge, and to pay her £100 for wearing it. An article by Albert Wolff in *Le Figaro* proved to be the finishing touch. On 27 June she answered: 'My dear Monsieur Wolff,. . . . if Paris is growing tired of the nonsense that is said about me, if they've decided to be frigid when I come home, I don't want to put them in a position where they have to do anything unworthy. I'm handing my resignation to the Comédie-Française.'

There was consternation. Letters flew to and fro between London and Paris. And while the agitated correspondence continued, Mme Bernhardt herself, 'the all too celebrated resigner,' had second thoughts, postponed her resignation, and gaily starred in a new and brilliant entertainment: the French Fête at the Royal Albert Hall. The Fête was arranged for 7 and 8 July in aid of the French Hospital in London. 'Who knows', cried a journalist, 'to what fabulous prices a

'The most exquisite example of the *fin de siècle Parisienne*.'
Sarah Bernhardt, *c.* 1900–3. From a gouache by Manuel Orazi.

GISMONDA

BERNHARDT

THÉÂTRE DE LA
RENAISSANCE

rose will rise when coming from the hands of Mlle Sarah Bernhardt?'
The Prince of Wales was expected on both days, the band of the Garde
Républicaine, despatched by the French Government, was to be 'con-
veyed without charge to London and back by the two Kentish railway
companies.' The Fête did not belie such enthusiasm. The Prince of
Wales bought a portrait of Sarah, and the royal party lingered a long
while at the stall where she 'laboured indefatigably all the afternoon,
haranguing, writing, raising the price upon her admirers, till she had
taken the largest earnings of any stall – £256. . . . The Prince of Wales
threw down a handful of notes to settle his accounts as he left. "*Il a
été très généreux,*" was the verdict.' One cannot help wondering if her
success with the Prince was already personal.

The Comédie gave its last performance on 12 July. Sarah returned
to Paris, and Perrin arrived at the avenue de Villiers in paternal and
conciliating mood. There was no question of her resignation. On 2
August, the Comédie-Française paid their birthday tribute to Molière.
Two by two, the actors came on stage, bearing palm or wreath to
decorate the bust of the dramatist. Sarah chose to come on stage alone.
She did not, like her colleagues, bow or curtsey. She advanced to the
footlights, and gazed resolutely into the eyes of Paris. A tremor ran
through the audience. Then, suddenly, there was a roar of acclamation.

Sarah was not to make many more entrances on the first stage of
France. On 17 April 1880, she played the part of Clorinde in *L'Aventurière*. She despised the part and the play, and she detested the author,
Émile Augier. On the eve of the performance she asked Perrin to postpone it for a week. She had been ill and unable to study for three days.
She had not even tried on her costumes. Perrin refused to postpone
the performance. The result was disastrous. 'You have only to see her
eccentric costume', snapped *Le Journal des Débats*, 'to see clearly that
she had an imperfect understanding of her part. Her gestures and
general appearance lacked nobility. . . . Let us be frank: in her outbursts in the third act, she was quite detestable.' At one moment in
the play, when Sarah leant over a candle, the audience were afraid
she would set light to her hair; next day a paper declared she had
wanted to set it on fire to stop the play before her utter failure. *Le Figaro*
administered the unkindest cut of all and declared her vulgar.

This time the break with the Comédie was final. 'It is my first failure
with the Comédie-Française,' Sarah wrote to Perrin. 'It will be my last.'

'The Comédie-Française', wrote Banville, 'does not know why Mlle

Sarah Bernhardt as Gismonda, 1894. This poster for
the Sardou play was one of the most famous to be designed
by Alphonse Mucha (1860–1939).

Sarah Bernhardt has left it, and Mlle Sarah Bernhardt does not know why she has left the Comédie-Française.' One of the reasons may have been the enmity of Augier; and no doubt Perrin, overwrought by her countless escapades, was glad when she departed. Years later an English admirer, Sir George Arthur, expressed his pleasure that Sarah had left the rue de Richelieu. If she had stayed, 'Princess Far-Away might never have carried her crimson roses; Izeyl would not have worn her orchid crown. And for his *Dame aux camélias* Dumas would surely have looked in vain for a star to shine between La Doche and La Duse, and in sheer beauty to outshine them both.' An English critic, A. B. Walkley, considered that London had played a large part in Sarah's decision. 'It was the extraordinary, the exaggerated, the unreasoning fuss that we made over her in London in 1879 that suggested to her soul to become like a star and dwell apart. It was the Gaiety French Play season of 1879 that turned Sarah Bernhardt into Sarah Barnum.'

The break was inevitable, but it was London that had taught Sarah Bernhardt her powers, given her her freedom. And she was too original, too tempestuous, too variable, too fired with a love of a measureless art, of universal travel and international glory, and (one must admit it) too much of an egoist to restrict herself to the rue de Richelieu. Thirty years later, in her memoirs, she herself confessed: 'That first evening in London decided my future.'

However, she had engaged herself to the Comédie for twenty years, and her contract still had fifteen years to run. She was ordered to pay 100,000 francs in damages. And over the next twenty years, whenever she had been on a fruitful tour, she would pay off part of her debt. In 1900, when she had paid some 70,000 francs, the theatre in the rue de Richelieu was burnt, and the Comédie found themselves homeless. Sarah offered them her own theatre on the most generous terms, and Jules Claretie, the administrator, cancelled the remainder of her debt.

Did Sarah ever regret the Comédie-Française? Perhaps she did. Certainly Claretie tried to re-engage her. On 16 May 1892 she called on him to discuss her re-engagement, and he offered her what had been given to Coquelin, the best-paid *sociétaire*: 40,000 francs. Sarah was accustomed by then to her world-wide tours and fabulous receipts. She found the sum far too small. Besides, as she explained, she had her own company; she might be going to Scandinavia. She did not want to be tied to the Comédie for three years. She could only stay for a year. Perhaps in a year's time she would change her mind. Claretie listened

Sarah Bernhardt as Lady Macbeth, 1884.

sadly to her torrent of excuses; but he noted in his diary that when she left she had a melancholy air.

But in April 1880, when Sarah left the Comédie, she was far from melancholy. She called on Dumas *fils* and asked him for *La Dame aux camélias*. 'The play is yours,' he answered. 'Do what you will with it.'

It was at this opportune moment that Jarrett re-appeared.

That man was an extraordinary man [wrote Sarah]. He was then sixty-five to seventy. Tall. The face of King Agamemnon, crowned with silver hair. . . . His eyes were blue; they were so pale that, when they blazed in anger, he seemed blind. . . .

That man was terrible. He was endowed with remarkable intelligence. He had had to struggle with life since he was a child, and he had conceived a deep scorn for humanity. He had suffered much himself, and he had no pity for those who suffered, because he said that every man was armed to defend himself. He had compassion for women, but did not love them. . . .

Jarrett was formidable. Immune to Sarah's charm, ignoring her caprices, he was the only man who earned her trust and her unswerving respect. Now, again, he asked her to sign a contract for America; and this time he mentioned details: 5000 francs for each performance, and half the receipts should the box office draw in a further 15,000. He offered her 1000 francs a week for hotels, and a special Pullman for her railway journeys, containing a bedroom with a four-poster bed, a salon complete with piano, four beds for her staff, and two chefs. He himself would take ten per cent of all she received.

She agreed to everything. Jarrett sent for Abbey, the American impresario; Abbey rushed from the New World to the Old. The contract was signed, and Sarah ordered twenty-five everyday dresses, six costumes for *Adrienne Lecouvreur*, four costumes for *Hernani*, and one for *Phèdre* (this alone cost 4000 francs). And then, to fill in time, she signed a contract with Mayer and Hollingshead for an intermediate season in London.

On 24 May, when Sarah began her second Gaiety season, she shone in a theatrical firmament which was resplendent with stars. At the Lyceum a few yards away Henry Irving and Ellen Terry were playing in *The Merchant of Venice*; at Covent Garden, Patti was singing in *Don Giovanni*; and at the Opéra Comique, every evening, the expectant crowd assembled to revel in 'a new and original opera, by Messrs W. S. Gilbert and Arthur Sullivan, *The Pirates of Penzance*.'

It was, then, a critical audience that assembled that summer evening for Sarah Bernhardt, an audience accustomed to good theatre. And many of them, again, recalled Rachel; for it was in *Adrienne Lecouvreur*, which Sarah would play for the first time that night, that Sarah's great predecessor had 'for the first time crossed the well-marked line separating classic tragedy from modern drama.' 'No doubt', considered the critic, 'it is easy to conceive passion that should present more dignity and self-restraint, till it flashed out in some supreme revelation. This was possible and natural to Rachel, but it is not thus that Mlle Bernhardt renders the emotion of such a scene. In her case physical as well as emotional abandonment is the dominant note of love. But the audience yielded to its charm, and by the end of the act the actress had regained her empire of the public.' She conquered them not only by charm, but by horrifying realism. The death of Adrienne Lecouvreur was considered one of Sarah's masterpieces. It was realistic to a degree which was rare even for her. It was a death by poison, and the effects of the poison could be seen. When, at last, she died, the audience burst into wild applause. Sarah did not achieve this triumph without suffering. Once, when she had prolonged her agony on stage, she almost collapsed in her dressing-room and only revived with the aid of smelling-salts. 'It's like that', muttered a colleague, 'nearly every time she acts this blessed play.'

Meanwhile, in London, in the summer of 1880, Sarah discarded the rôle of the eighteenth-century actress and appeared as the social butterfly in *Frou-Frou*. It, too, proved to be a triumph for her. The most cordial appreciation came from Francisque Sarcey, who once again had bustled across the Channel to report on Sarah's activities abroad. The moment *Frou-Frou* was over, he scurried to her dressing-room. 'Well,' he said to her, 'if you want it, this evening will re-open the doors of the Comédie-Française.' 'Don't mention that again,' she replied.

Sarah Bernhardt's second Gaiety season ended on 19 June. She had re-conquered London. And London, over the years, was to make the admitted conquest of Sarah. For London, so she came to write,

... is a special city. Only very slowly is its charm revealed.... But, little by little, the profusion of squares, the beauty of the aristocratic women effaces for ever the image of the flower-sellers. The dizzying movement of Hyde Park, and, above all, of Rotten Row fills the mind with gaiety. Generous hospitality undoes the stiffness of the first handshake. The wit of Englishmen may be compared without disadvantage with the wit of Frenchmen; and the gallantry,

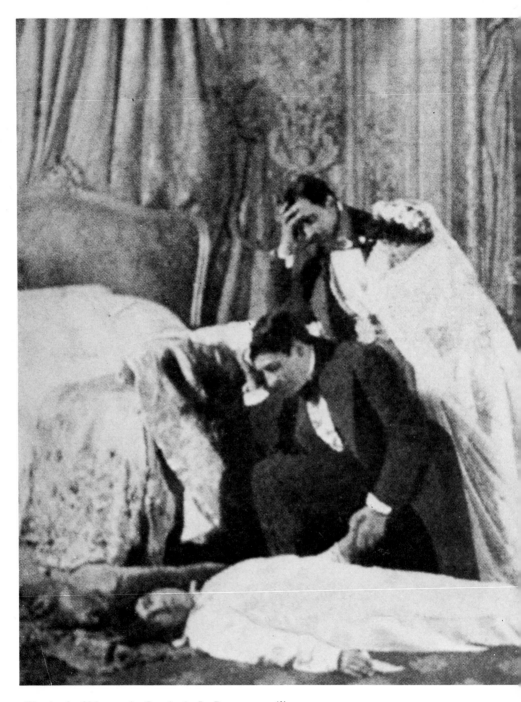

The death of Marguerite Gautier in *La Dame aux camélias*.
'Madame, madame,' said the future Queen Alexandra to Sarah,
'how glad I am to see you alive again after the fifth act!'

much more respectful, and so much more flattering, does not make one regret the proverbial gallantry of the French. . . .

Now [she wrote at the turn of the century] I adore the city of London and, I need hardly say, its inhabitants. Since I first went there with the Comédie, I have been back a score of times; and the public has always been faithful, even fond of me.

Sarah stayed a few days in Paris on her return; then (for she needed money to pay for the Comédie) she left for Brussels, then for Copenhagen. In Copenhagen the Director of the Theatre Royal, the King's First Chamberlain, boarded the train to greet her, the police were forced to clear a way for her carriage, and the waiting multitudes threw her kisses and flowers. The first night was attended by the King and Queen, the King and Queen of the Hellenes, and the Princess of Wales, and the two queens tossed her their bouquets. Sarah had much reverence for historical traditions and for the august sovereigns and princes whom she met. She frankly admitted in later years that the finest day in her life was the day on which she was summoned to Nice to play before Queen Victoria. But, of all the illustrious personages whom she came to know, one figure always appealed to her irresistibly. In Copenhagen she was presented to the then Princess of Wales. 'Oh! what an adorable and entrancing face! The eyes of a child of the North in a Greek face of virginal purity, a long slender neck made for the greeting of a queen, and a gentle, almost timid smile. The indefinable charm of this princess made her so luminous that I saw nobody else but her.' The friendship of the future Queen Alexandra was (according to Sir George Arthur) 'one of the happiest items' in Sarah Bernhardt's life.

Now, when she asked to visit Elsinore, Christian ix offered her a boat, and, escorted by a constellation of Danish celebrities, she visited Hamlet's tomb and drank from Ophelia's well. Next day after her performance the King invested her with the Decoration for Merit, in diamonds. It seemed that nothing could interrupt her idyll. And nothing would have done so, had not Baron Magnus, the Prussian Minister, risen to give a toast at the farewell dinner, a toast 'to France, which gives us such great artists, to France, the land of beauty beloved by us all.'

It was hardly a decade since Sarah had nursed the wounded at the Odéon; since the Prussian regiments had marched down the Champs-Élysées; since Alsace and Lorraine had been lost to France. 'I am French,' Sarah Bernhardt was to say, 'I am French by birth, at heart,

Ophelia: a bas-relief
by Sarah Bernhardt.

in spirit, art and love.' The Minister had hardly finished speaking when
she rose and cried: 'So be it, Your Excellency! Let us drink to France,
but to the whole of France!' The Court orchestra struck up the Marseillaise; the room became deserted as if by magic.

Next morning Sarah was summoned to see an attaché from the
French Legation. He gave her a draft explanation to sign, but she
rejected it. The Press and the public, both anti-German, cheered her
wholeheartedly when she drove to the station. 'We had Sarah Bernhardt performing here,' wrote the critic and philosopher, Georg
Brandes, 'and the city has talked of nothing else this week.'

On 15 October 1880, Sarah Bernhardt boarded the *Amérique* and set
out, like Rachel before her, to conquer the New World.

95

On 27 October the *Amérique* stopped in an icebound Hudson River. The icebreakers hewed a way for the ship to dock, and three small boats sailed out to greet Doña Sol. Then the crowd of admirers, sightseers and reporters burst on board. American publicity, and Sarah's American legend, had begun.

On 8 November she gave her first performance at Booth's Theatre in *Adrienne Lecouvreur*. New York was conquered; and when she returned that night to her hotel she found a crowd assembled to serenade her. In *La Dame aux camélias* she was, they said, the greatest of Marguerites; and in *Phèdre*, when she was still and silent, there was the smell of sulphur in the air, proclaiming that, though the crash had not come, it was coming – it was there.

When she arrived at the theatre for her last New York performance she found the street blocked by admirers. One woman took off an amethyst brooch and pinned it to Sarah's cloak; another enthusiast, trying to snip a lock off her hair, only cut an expensive feather off her Parisian hat. That night after the curtain fell Sarah went by special train to visit Thomas Edison. At two o'clock on a moonless morning they arrived at Menlo Park. Then Sarah, lulled by the warmth of her furs, and the swaying of the carriage, was woken from her dreams by a formidable cheer. The countryside suddenly lit up, and the carriage bowled down the illuminated drive and drew up at Edison's door. 'When he had done us the honours of his telephonic discoveries and his astonishing phonograph,' wrote Sarah, 'Edison gave me his arm and led me to the dining-room, where I found his family assembled. I was very tired, and I did justice to the supper which had been prepared with such good grace.' Sarah was charmed by Edison's courtesy, by his love of Shakespeare, and by his likeness to Napoleon, and she marvelled at his inventions. At four o'clock she left again for Boston.

From Boston she crossed the frontier and went to Montreal; the Bernhardt train steamed in on a night so cold that her huge bouquet was crystallized. And the shivering Doña Sol who stood in the light of a hundred lanterns held by a hundred students to hear an ode of welcome in eight stanzas, collapsed with cold in the midst of her admirers. The Bishop of Montreal forbade his flock from the pulpit to see the sinful woman on stage. 'My dear colleague,' answered Sarah, 'why attack me so violently? Actors ought not to be hard on one another.' As for the Bishop of Chicago – when they recrossed the frontier – his denunciation of Sarah Bernhardt aroused so much interest in the prospective

Thomas Edison in his laboratory. From a photograph. Sarah was charmed by Edison's likeness to Napoleon, and she marvelled at his inventions.

performance in his diocese that Abbey sent the poor of Chicago $200, which otherwise he would have spent on advertising.

The show went on. New Orleans, Mobile, Memphis, Louisville, Cincinnati, Columbus: through them all steamed the train, and Doña Sol on a rocking-chair on the platform of her carriage saw the panorama of endless plains and forests ever changing. Dayton, Indianapolis, St Joseph, Leavenworth, Quincy, Springfield. . . . The train puffed on its way. Chicago, Detroit, Cleveland, Pittsburgh, Bradford and Erie, over the frontier they went to perform at Toronto; back again they went to Buffalo, Rochester and Utica. Then off to Washington (where they had supper at the French Embassy), Baltimore and Philadelphia. Finally, and breathlessly, they returned to New York. Mark Twain was to tell the story of two young New Yorkers who had struggled to save enough dollars to see Sarah Bernhardt. On their way to the theatre, they met two beggar women, and they were so touched by their poverty that they handed them the money. The beggars did not spend this windfall on clothes or even bread: they went to the theatre to see Sarah.

Sarah bade farewell to America with *La Dame aux camélias*, and she took fourteen curtain calls. On 4 May she embarked in the *Amérique* for France.

On 6 June 1881 the Gymnase company opened their London season at the Gaiety, 'to be reinforced in a few days by Mlle Sarah Bernhardt.' She made her entrance on 11 June in *La Dame aux camélias*, a play which, in America, had brought her endless offers of marriage and countless cures for consumption: a play which the Victorians enjoyed with prudish pleasure. Though the Lord Chamberlain sanctioned it in French, though sung in Italian it was openly applauded, it was in fact proscribed in any English version; and 'the crowded and brilliant audience, including the Prince and Princess of Wales,' watched Sarah that night with all the pleasure of Adam enjoying forbidden fruit. 'Time after time', wrote Sarcey, 'she cast into the part the poetry that her predecessors had forgotten to put there.' 'You play the part with modesty,' Queen Victoria was to tell her, 'and no one can complain.'

It was, it seems, on her return that Sarah fell headlong in love.

Ambroise Aristide Damala was the fifth child of Ambroise Damala and Calliope (known as *la belle Damala*), daughter of Lucas Ralli, sometime Mayor of Piraeus. He was born on 6 January 1855. The Damalas were

On 4 April 1882, at St. Andrew's, Wells Street, London,
Sarah Bernhardt married Ambroise Aristide Damala. . . .

an aristocratic family, and they lived in Syra, one of the islands of the
Aegean. In about 1860 they had moved to Marseilles where the elder
Damala established himself in business. Ambroise Aristide was edu-
cated first in Marseilles and later at the Collège Royal de Louis-le-
Grand in Paris. In 1869 M. Damala died, leaving some 300,000 francs
to each child. Aristide became an adventurer. He was the handsomest
subaltern in the Greek cavalry, and one of the bravest in the war of
1875–8. At one time he served with the Foreign Legion in the Sahara.
He studied to be a diplomat, and finally came to Paris where he spent
the last thousand francs of his inheritance, and soon involved himself,
it is said, in numerous intrigues. His Oriental parties, wrote Mme Berton, the actor's wife, at which the guests 'divested themselves of their

PUNCH'S FANCY PORTRAITS.—No. 79.

THE TRANSIT OF THE CONSTELLATION SARA.

BRILLIANT SCENE IN A CIRCLE, OR "RAPID ACT," WITH WHICH THIS
VARIOUSLY GIFTED *ARTISTE* HAS SUCCESSFULLY TERMINATED HER
LATEST, SHORTEST, AND MOST IMPORTANT ENGAGEMENT, WHEN SHE
TEMPORARILY QUITTED THE STAGE FOR THE SAKE OF THE MASTER OF
THE RING. THIS SEASON WE SHALL WELCOME *LA DAME*,—NO, *LA
DAMALA AUX CAMÉLIAS!* OR THEY MIGHT APPEAR IN A FRENCH
VERSION OF *THE HAPPY PAIR* AND THE OLD FARCE OF *SARAH'S
YOUNG MAN.*

On 15 April the marriage was duly recorded
in *Punch*.

clothing and plunged naked into baths of champagne', were the talk
of Paris. Perhaps Damala was already a victim of morphine; and perhaps it was in the world of drug-addicts that he met Sarah's half-sister,
Jeanne.

Was it Jeanne, or was it Delaunay, the actor, who introduced him
to Sarah? We cannot tell. But Delaunay gave him drama lessons, and
one September morning in 1881 Damala called at the avenue de
Villiers. Sarah found herself in the presence of 'a tall and handsome
man with a pair of ferocious mustachios' and no acting experience. He
boldly asked for a part, and she told him to learn Don Carlos' mono-
logue in *Hernani* and to recite it to her three days hence. Three days
later she engaged him, asked him to learn the rest of the part and to

100

play it with her in Brussels. And so it was that Damala first appeared on stage in *Hernani*, in Belgium, in the autumn of 1881. The tour continued in triumph through Vienna and St Petersburg, Warsaw, Genoa, Basle and Lausanne, Lyons and Trieste. By the time they performed in Naples on 31 March 1882 Sarah was playing opposite her fiancé.

Perhaps it is true that she found herself a rival in love of the actress Jane Hading, and wanted to secure her passion. Perhaps, at thirty-seven, she felt the need for lasting love. More probably she was attracted by Damala's indifference. Sarah was always inspired by resistance, and he alone of all the men she had known had not been immediately conquered. 'I made up my mind to marry him,' she told a reporter years later; and, being Sarah, she had to be satisfied at once. Since French and Italian laws imposed delays on marriage, she and Damala had to be married in England; and since he was an orthodox Greek and she was a Catholic, and neither the Greek nor the Roman Church allowed marriage in mid-Lent, they had to be married in a Protestant church.

They paid a flying visit to London; and on 4 April the assistant curate at St Andrew's, Wells Street, married a young man of twenty-seven 'who resembled Mounet-Sully, but was better looking,' and a woman of thirty-seven, very pale and fatigued with her journey, and wearing, said *The Morning Post*, 'a dress *vieil or*, and a bonnet de Loutre, with a pearl and gold ornament.'

M. and Mme Damala left that night from Charing Cross on their way to Barcelona. Mme Damala was to play in Madrid that Saturday.

It was, of course, a thronged theatre that greeted her when, on 25 May, after visits to Portugal, Spain and Switzerland, she reappeared in Paris to perform in *La Dame aux camélias* opposite her husband. Often as Paris had seen her on the stage with her current lover, this evening presented her in a more dramatic light. Small wonder that this charity performance of Dumas' play proved to be 'the greatest success that a Parisian manager could attempt.' 'I paid 25 louis for my box,' said one satisfied spectator, 'but I cried enough for 2000 francs.'

A few days later, with the same play, Sarah opened her new London season, and Damala made his first appearance on the London stage. Was he for a moment inspired by his wife? Or did London applaud, like Paris, from sentimentality? An admiring critic decided that 'the part of Armand was played by M. Damala with a surprising degree of confidence and finish, considering that he has only been six months on the stage.'

Sarah Bernhardt – again by Alphonse Mucha. This poster was designed for *la Journée Sarah Bernhardt*, 9 December 1896. It shows Sarah wearing the tiara of lilies which she had worn as Mélissinde, in *La Princesse lointaine*.

EN
L'HONNEUR
de
SARAH BERNHARDT
ses admirateurs et ses amis

IMPRIMÉ POUR "L'ÉDITION D'ART" PAR F. CHAMPEO

E. Mesplès

It was on one of her frequent visits to London that the Queen of the French theatre was the guest of the reigning monarch of the English stage. Henry Irving, always conscious of his regal status, felt it incumbent upon him to extend an almost official welcome to distinguished foreign actors passing through London. These receptions were given in the Beefsteak Room of the Lyceum Theatre. After the last rehearsal of *Henry VIII* he gave a supper in honour of Sarah Bernhardt. During supper that night, Sarah leaned across the table to Ellen Terry and said: 'My darling, there are two people who shall never be old – you and I.'

How wonderful she looked in those days [Ellen Terry remembered]! She was as transparent as an azalea, only more so: like a cloud, only not so thick. Smoke from a burning paper describes her more nearly! She was hollow-eyed, thin, almost consumptive-looking. Her body was not the prison of her soul, but its shadow.

On the stage she has always seemed to me a symbol, an ideal, an epitome rather than a *woman*. It is this quality which makes her so easy in such lofty parts as Phèdre. She is always a miracle. . . . It is this extraordinary decorative and symbolic quality of Sarah's which makes her transcend all personal and individual feeling on the stage. No-one plays a love-scene better, but it is a *picture* of love that she gives, a strange orchidaceous picture rather than a suggestion of the ordinary human passion as felt by ordinary people. She is exotic. Well, what else could she be?

She could also be astonishing. In 1883 she played the title-part in Sardou's *Fédora*. The Prince of Wales, who was in Paris, called on her in her dressing-room. He said that he would have liked to be an actor. Sarah took him at his word and dressed him up. That night, when Fédora discovered the corpse of Vladimir and threw herself on her knees beside the death-bed, her *Vladimir adoré* was Albert Edward, Prince of Wales.

Sarah was autocratic. She was insatiable. And she was infinitely alluring. No one disputed the crown with her. Her enemies and critics, like her myriad admirers, watched her with fascination.

Wider still, and wider, the bounds of legend were set. There were graphic accounts of the 'nicely polished skeleton' admiring itself in the glass in her bedroom. There was certainly a skull inscribed by Victor Hugo. There were yet more tales of the coffin embellished with her initials and with her defiant motto *Quand même*: the coffin in which she was said to study her parts. It was rumoured that Sarah was plotting

Sarah Bernhardt in *La Tosca*, 1888.

OPPOSITE 'She was so endowed', wrote Théodore de Banville, 'that whatever she might do she was absolutely and unconsciously lyrical.' Sarah Bernhardt's poetic beauty is seen in this early photograph.

RIGHT Prince of Wales, later Edward VII. Legend says that, in 1883, when Sarah played Fédora, he once played the corpse of her *Vladimir adoré*.

to restore the Empire. It was said that she drank enormously, that she had ordered a coach in gold and ebony, that she was not a woman at all, but a boy masquerading in woman's clothes. The stories about her thinness were innumerable. It was alleged that when she made ascensions by balloon she entered by a spiral staircase inside the rope; that when it rained she kept dry by passing between the falling drops.

It is one of the stranger rewards of fame to find oneself recorded in fiction; and when in 1880 the curtain of the Vaudeville rose on Alphonse Daudet's play, *Le Nabab*, the studio of Félicia Ruys, with its sculpture, its *objets d'art*, its gambolling greyhound, Kadour, was soon recognized as a replica of Sarah's studio. Sarah herself was the subject of more than one novel. Later in life she was to record much autobiography in that strange, ill-written amalgam of fact and fiction, *Petite Idole*; now, in 1882, she was the unmistakable heroine of a *roman à clef* by Félicien Champsaur: *Dinah Samuel*.

Champsaur portrayed her vividly as she appeared to his hero, Patrice Montclar, in the avenue de Villiers. She inspired Montclar with one of the finest verbal portraits painted of her: a portrait that repeats and enlarges that exquisite photograph taken in early years.

She sat down, near the window with the Gothic glass, white and yellow, in a monumental carved oak chair. A tall palm-tree stretched its pointed leaves overhead. On the mantelpiece an oil lamp burned with a flame kept low, casting a great shadow on the ceiling.... In this dim light, gentle as starlight, Dinah Samuel was wonderful, so fine was her wild-seeming hair, so caressing the gaze of her damson eyes through their long lashes, so crimson were her lips and such their smile, so fascinating were the eyes. At moments he saw nothing but the actress's eyes. They grew into lakes that were large enough to drown him....

One of her hands was resting on the arm of the chair, the other toyed with a cambric handkerchief trimmed with lace. She was draped in a dress of cream brocade fastened with a large band of ermine.... A snow-coloured ribbon, its wide ends floating loose, tied a bunch of white lilac at her breast, a posy held by a golden lizard with emerald eyes. From the high lace collar, *à la* Marie Stuart, the supple body, swathed in its ermine-bordered brocade, drew undulating lines to the feet. And the feet were shod with white satin slippers embroidered with mother-of-pearl flowers, and enhanced by silver heels....

The year 1882 brought Sarah not only the role of Dinah Samuel, not only the new role of a wife, but that of a director of a theatre. Some time ago she had agreed to open her new season at the Vaudeville in

'She has been queen, she has been woman. She has been all women. . . .'
Sarah Bernhardt, photographed by Nadar.

Sardou's *Fédora*; and now, despite her entreaties, Sardou refused to have Damala as Fédora's lover. It was a hard decision to break to a husband who was already envious and bitter: a man who was perhaps even now a confirmed morphine addict. Sarah solved the problem by commissioning *Les Mères ennemies* from Catulle Mendès. It was a play with a fine part for Damala. She appealed to her husband's pride, and pointed out the advantage of taking an undisputed lead rather than an obvious second place. Then, in her anxiety to keep him, she leased the Théâtre de l'Ambigu regardless of the probable financial loss. In a further attempt to placate her son, who still firmly opposed the marriage, she leased the theatre under the name of Maurice Bernhardt.

On 17 November *Les Mères ennemies* had its first successful performance. On 11 December the opening of *Fédora* at the Vaudeville marked the beginning of the collaboration between Sarah and that skilful, prolific dramatist, Victorien Sardou. Just as Bizet had composed *Carmen* to suit Galli-Marié, Sardou had written *Fédora* to suit Sarah. Maurice Baring, seeing Eleonora Duse in the part, recognized that it had been 'made like a tight-fitting garment for Sarah Bernhardt, and we have never seen another artist who could wear it.' Sarah herself found the part very hard; but that evening, in Paris, the god descended. Her feline charm, her violence sent a shudder through the audience. In the fourth act, when Sardou had arranged for Fédora to die of poison, her pathos was superb; and *faire sa Sarah* became the accepted phrase for dying dramatically. 'The electric, chimerical woman had once again conquered Paris,' wrote the critic Jules Lemaître. 'With *Fédora* we found the real Sarah again, the Sarah unique and all-powerful, she who is not content to sing, but lives and vibrates through and through.'

Sarah saw herself triumph with mixed emotions. It was hard to know how her husband would receive this victory which eclipsed his own achievement at the Ambigu. She had not long to wait. On 16 December, after a fierce quarrel, he accused her of trying to ruin his stage career, and abruptly left the avenue de Villiers.

In February 1883 he suddenly returned. His physical condition was now worsening; and one day in April, in sorrow and in fury, Sarah threw away all the morphine and syringes she could find. Damala left the house again, and she obtained a legal separation. She sought consolation, not for the first time, in the arms of a burly, bearded poet, the antithesis of Damala: Jean Richepin.

It was with Richepin that, in June, she returned to Copenhagen. The

'Sarah, the divine, was here in Copenhagen with her shadow, Jean Richepin,' wrote a Danish critic in 1883. Richepin, poet and dramatist (1849–1926), consoled Sarah Bernhardt for her legal separation from Damala.

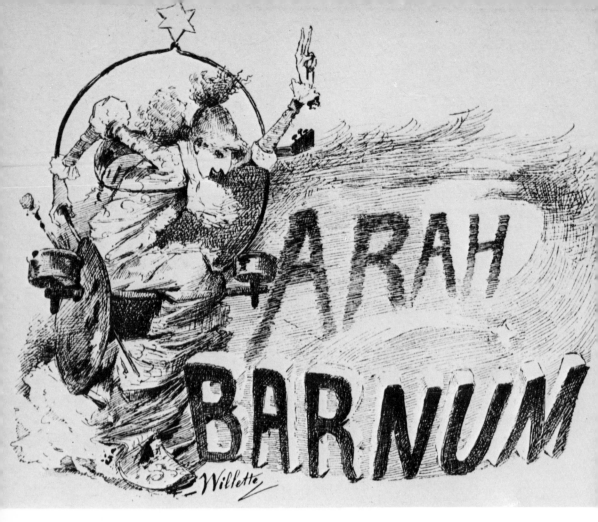

This cover was designed by Willette for Marie Colombier's
scurrilous book about Sarah Bernhardt, 1883.

city was so festive in her honour that some inhabitants, unaware of what
was happening, asked if the excitement meant a change of government.
From Copenhagen they went to Stockholm, where King Oscar
attended all her five performances and awarded her a gold medal and
a crown of brilliants inscribed *Literis et artibus*. Yet it was perhaps in
London that Sarah felt herself to be most surely the empress of the stage;
and on 9 July, at a Gaiety Theatre resplendent with the new electric
light, she opened a one-week season in *Fédora*.

Before the year was over, the curtain had risen upon a real and more
resounding drama. Jeanne Bernhardt, a morphine addict, had not been
well enough to set off with Sarah on her American tour; and she had
been obliged to join the company when the tour was under way. Sarah

had therefore engaged a friend of long standing to replace her: an actress, popular on the boulevards, by the name of Marie Colombier. Marie Colombier had published a vivid account of the tour: *Le Voyage de Sarah Bernhardt en Amérique.* It was, apparently, after this publication that Marie and Sarah quarrelled violently; and Marie, betraying her intimate friendship, published a scabrous biography whose heroine was clear from the title *Les Mémoires de Sarah Barnum.*

Marie Colombier described how the youthful Sarah had become a courtesan 'for whom all the marriage vows were contained in a well-filled wallet'. She recalled how Sarah became the mistress of de Véranne (a cross, it seems, between Kératry and the Prince de Ligne); she mentioned the birth of Loris (a thin disguise for Maurice). Sarah Barnum, she wrote, had

... a strange power of seduction which put an army of faithful admirers at her feet, but could not make a single worshipper bow down before her altar. . . . Unable to conquer a man, she wanted . . . to conquer all men. . . . The Barnum's charm was a studied charm, a calculated charm, a settled determination. And what made her powerful was that she did not scorn anything or anyone. She would have made a great politician. She would have inspired fanaticisms like Bonaparte, devotions like Maria Theresa. . . . Unfortunately, she knew how to attract, but not how to keep. Her acts of violence, her whims, her fantastic caprices, her cold-blooded malice killed all fanaticisms, all devotions. These were revived or replaced, thanks to her charm, but her house was never a home: it was a passage.

And then, most wickedly, Marie Colombier described Sarah Barnum's pursuit of Jack Madaly, 'an improvised actor. This Madaly was a handsome fellow – "a male," said Barnum. He was a fine specimen of the Oriental type . . .' Marie Colombier suggested Madaly's preference for another actress; and she described how Sarah Barnum, blind drunk with half a bottle of absinthe, had fallen down, fractured her skull and died.

Sarah Bernhardt took the law into her own hands. She and Richepin called on Marie Colombier; and Sarah, never mild in her emotions,

... laid a whip across her face with all the strength she was able to command. The authoress of *Sarah Barnum* fled. She ran from room to room all over the flat. Sarah Bernhardt followed, smashing as she pursued every knick-knack and piece of bric-à-brac she could lay hands on. She looked [said *The Daily News*] like a destroying angel in the midst of broken furniture, china, pictures, and glass. Marie Colombier escaped eventually by the back stairs. . . . Notwithstanding the emotions of the afternoon, the accomplished actress went in the evening to rehearse *Nana Sahib*.

Nana Sahib was set in India at the time of the Mutiny of 1857. Marais played Nana Sahib, the Indian chief, and Sarah played Djamma, his fierce, voluptuous mistress. Alas, even Sarah's gifts could not save the melodrama; and when Marais fell ill and, at Sarah's desperate request, Richepin himself, with no acting experience, took over the part of Nana Sahib, the play was doomed. Even the attraction of seeing her current lover with her on the stage could not make the play run to forty performances.

This failure was all the more cruel to Sarah because Damala had now been cured, and he had returned independently to the theatre. On 15 December, two hundred yards from the Porte-Saint-Martin, he opened at the Gymnase in the title rôle of *Le Maître des forges*, a part which seemed to be made expressly for him. *Le Maître des forges* was based on an immensely successful novel by Georges Ohnet; it ran for over three hundred performances.

The failure of Richepin's *Nana Sahib* and of his crude prose version of *Macbeth* in May 1884 were to weaken his liaison with Sarah, and he went the way of all her lovers. But Sarah was never long unattended, and her new worshipper soon made his entrance. It might be more true to say that an old lover had returned. On 26 December 1884, a year to the day after she had appeared with Richepin in *Nana Sahib*, she appeared with Philippe Garnier in *Théodora*.

Théodora was Sardou's greatest triumph with Sarah: indeed, it was one of the greatest triumphs in her career. It was the story of the ex-dancer taken to wife by the Emperor Justinian. Under the name of Théodora she remained a courtesan, only to learn one day that her current lover meant to assassinate the Emperor and Empress. Justinian discovered the plot and his wife's infidelity, and Théodora was put to death. 'Heaven', wrote Jules Lemaître, 'has endowed Mme Sarah Bernhardt with singular gifts. . . . And Mme Sarah Bernhardt marvellously exploits this air of a fairy-tale princess, of a chimerical and far-away creature. . . . In the first act, lying on her bed, the mitre on her brow, a great lily in her hand, she looks like the fantastic queens of Gustave Moreau, those dream-figures by turn hieratic and serpentine, of a mystic and sensual attraction.'

Théodora was renowned as much for its Byzantine splendour as for

its action. The costumes worn by the palace guards (observed a dazzled journalist) cost over 300 francs apiece; even those of the eunuchs cost 125 francs. In the scene set in the Imperial box at the Hippodrome, Sarah wore a dress of sky-blue satin with a train four yards long, covered with embroidered peacocks with ruby eyes and feathers of emeralds and sapphires.

Small wonder that *Théodora* was performed more than three hundred times, with a single break in the summer of 1885, when the Empress Sarah took the play to London.

Late in April 1886, with Garnier in attendance, Sarah embarked at Bordeaux for a tour of more than a year.

She travelled with her company in special trains and steamers, accompanied by a numerous suite, by her favourite animals, and by uncountable pieces of luggage. Eighty cases were not enough for her

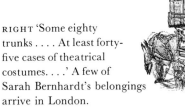

RIGHT 'Some eighty trunks . . . . At least forty-five cases of theatrical costumes. . . .' A few of Sarah Bernhardt's belongings arrive in London.

SOME OF THE LUGGAGE

dresses and hats, and shoes, her linen and scent, and her personal baubles and trinkets. 'When someone comes to write the poem of those world tours,' said Edmond Rostand, 'to describe all the décors and characters, the beauties and the oddities, to record the dialogues of loco-motives and steamers, to chronicle the speech and song and shouting of the choirs of poets and savages, kings and exotic animals, he will have to be some unheard-of Homer composed of a Théophile Gautier, a Jules Verne and a Rudyard Kipling.'

For the first time Sarah visited South America. In Rio de Janeiro Dom Pedro II, Emperor of Brazil, came to every performance. 'Absurdly rich men, wearing black whiskers and covered with jewels,

OPPOSITE This photograph by Nadar shows
Sarah Bernhardt, again in the title-rôle of *Théodora*.
The play was written for her in 1884.

like idols, used to wait outside the stage-door, and lay their handkerchiefs on the ground so that the dust should not soil the feet of Théodora.' On 17 July Sarah made her début in Buenos Aires, where her twenty performances brought 80,000 spectators to gaze upon her, and the grateful Argentinians presented her with an estate of 13,000 acres. She spent eight days at Montevideo, a week at Valparaiso, four days at Santiago, and then went on to Lima for a brief season in Peru. September saw her in Havana. In Mexico she made 260,000 francs in ten performances, then travelled by way of Texas to the United States, resumed the American tour of five years earlier, and ended in New York in April 1887.

After an absence of thirteen months, with a profit of 800,000 francs and a tigress, Sarah returned to Europe; but not to rest, for by May she was in London and for the first time she toured England, Scotland and Ireland. She long remembered an experience which she had on her first tour in Scotland, 'that country where they are so pious that they do nothing on Sundays.' She had arrived in some remote town on a Sunday evening. There was no fire in her suite of rooms. Several times she asked for a fire, but the Scots did not intend to risk their salvation for any actress, least of all a French one. Finally, in desperation, Sarah rushed on to the landing and screamed 'Fire! Fire!' at the top of her voice. She cleared the hotel in two minutes.

Those were the days, recalled May Agate, when Sarah would burn up a suite of furniture and pay for it cheerfully rather than be cold. One suite in Spain had proved to be rather expensive. 'Mahogany doesn't burn very well,' Sarah had murmured.

In September 1887 Sarah stayed, for the first time, at Belle-Île-en-Mer.

It was on an excursion to Brittany that she had discovered La Pointe des Poulains at the very north of Belle-Île. It was a wild, forbidding place: on one side she could see the coast of Brittany, on the other side the vast expanse of sea. She was drawn by the sombre beauty of the cliffs, the lowering abandoned fort, with its loopholes and machicolations; and since, with Sarah, an idea must be realized at the moment of conception, she bought the grim block of masonry and the rocks and fields around it. It was here that Our Lady of Belle-Île came in summer to take a few weeks' rest among her friends.

There were so many friends that she had to buy more land and build annexes. First came a studio for the artist Georges Clairin. Then came

Madame de Belle-Île. Sarah Bernhardt at her island home off the coast of Brittany, 1903.

MADAME SARAH BERNHARDT
AT BELLE-ILE EN-MER.

Photographs by G. Chusseau-Flaviens, Paris. (See "Small Talk of the Week.")

"'FOR NOW I STAND AS ONE UPON A ROCK,
ENVIRONED WITH A WILDERNESS OF SEA.'"

Sarah Bernhardt fishing at Belle-Île, 1903.

five apartments called, respectively, Europe, Asia, Africa, America and Oceania. 'Where is Monsieur Maurice?' Sarah once enquired of her Secretary, Pitou. 'Monsieur Maurice is in Oceania, Madame. . . .' There were also, in time, the villa Lysiane and the villa Simone (named after her granddaughters), the villa l'Aiglon, and the farm, where Sarah liked to make cream and to play Marie-Antoinette.

At Belle-Île Sarah rose very early and went out to shoot sea-birds. She used to come back at eight o'clock, put down her gun, and set off again, this time to fish. At eleven o'clock she would return, have a bath, and dress for *déjeuner*, which was served at half-past twelve. One day at *déjeuner* they discussed precious stones.

'I have a horror of sad jewels, of sombre stones,' says Sarah. 'Jewels ought to be happy. . . . And I detest diamonds.'

We go through the precious stones [recorded Reynaldo Hahn]. Sarah enthuses about burnt topaz.

'It's deep, variegated, much finer than yellow diamonds.'

She likes turquoise 'against the skin' (in the evening, not during the day), and very bright sapphires; she adores pearls.

We talk about railways, accidents. She grows angry because third-class carriages are not so well protected against accidents as first-class carriages.

'It's infamous, infamous!'

Reynaldo Hahn (1874–1947): composer, friend of Proust,
and admirer of Sarah Bernhardt.

After *déjeuner*, protocol demanded a siesta. This was taken in the Sarahtorium: a sunlit spot which was planted, on Sarah's orders, with tamarisk trees. Inside the wall of tamarisks there were chaises-longues and garden tables. Here everyone continued to chat, and to comment on the newspaper articles and reviews which the postman had just brought. From time to time the guests got up to confirm the arrival of yet another contingent of tourists. Stationed on a distant hill, and armed with binoculars, Sarah's importunate admirers strained their eyes to catch a glimpse of her. Sarah herself shut her eyes and covered her face with a thick veil. From time to time she said: 'I'm asleep, I'm asleep!'

Suddenly she would 'wake up' and say that her siesta was over. They would all set off for a walk among the rocks, or visit the farm. Then they would go to Clairin's studio, a pavilion which consisted of a large room, a small bedroom, and a tiny bathroom where Clairin – Jojotte, she called him – took seaweed baths. These seaweed baths were much in vogue at Belle-Île, and everyone praised their vivifying, antiseptic and somniferous qualities. Reynaldo Hahn, on his summer visit, found Sarah, fresh from her seaweed bath, sunning herself on the roof of the fort. She was wearing a Japanese robe and a panama hat, and a green veil round her neck. She was lazing happily after fourteen months' continuous work.

Her idea of rest was relative. Every year she brought some forty manuscripts to Belle-Île, and chose the plays which she was to perform during the season.

At five o'clock, unfailingly, everyone assembled for tennis. It was difficult to play tennis with Sarah. She served well and returned with vigour; but, as she refused to move an inch, every ball had to be sent to the exact spot where she could return it without stirring. Maurice fulfilled her requirements to perfection. Hahn was so alarmed that he went into hiding in the summer-house where they kept the racquets. Here he dozed until a servant arrived with cold drinks, and told Sarah that there were snails in the kitchen. Despite the horrified protests of her guests, she commanded that the snails should be brought to her at once. She ate them on the tennis-court with relish. Then she went back to the fort in her little donkey-carriage.

It was time to dress for dinner. After dinner came conversation or music-making. Everyone retired to bed at ten o'clock.

In the intervals between such activities, Sarah continued her

sculpture. She created chimerical flowers in bronze, modelled the
curious salt-cellars, candelabra and paperweights, incrusted with glau-
cous ceramics, which were to be shown at the International Exhibition
of 1900. Reynaldo Hahn recorded a more macabre piece of sculpture:
the head of a drowned girl, clutched by a crab. This work was called
The Kiss of the Sea. But, however strange her taste, Sarah was intrigued
by the flora and fauna of the sea; and this efflorescence of bronzes, this
sculpture rich and strange, did not impede the progress of the actress
and the theatre director.

One of the most engaging accounts of Sarah at Belle-Île was given
by Yvonne Lanco, a friend of Sarah's granddaughter, Simone. Yvonne,
as a child, was taken by her parents to Les Poulains. She and Simone
stood in awe, together, by the cage of the great horn-owl, Alexis. The
bird grew fierce when they approached, for Sarah used to tease him,
and he mistrusted everyone. In the alley which led to the fort the children found two pelicans. These were at least six feet high, but there was
no need to be afraid: they were reassuringly made of wood.

Long after Sarah had bought the fort, she acquired the neighbouring

Service to order: Sarah Bernhardt
on the tennis-court at Belle-Île,
in her sixtieth year.

château of Penhoët. The château, built for the Comte du Houssoy, was a hideous building, and the red-tiled roof offended Our Lady of Belle-Île. 'Oh, if I had a cannon,' she muttered, 'how I should love to blow up that dreadful thing!' When the Comte du Houssoy died, Sarah was appalled to think that the château might become a hotel. She duly acquired it and, since it was more comfortable than the fort, she settled in it. She brought some fine furniture, but there were still improvements to make. The furniture in her bedroom was Breton, carved with figures in old-fashioned costumes. Sarah painted the furniture herself in the style of Quimper pottery. The dark oak vanished under a coat of white paint, and the figures and motifs were brightly coloured. Not content with interior decoration, Sarah determined to create a Mediterranean garden on the Atlantic coast. The climate of Belle-Île was so mild that mimosa and camellias flowered abundantly, and roses bloomed almost throughout the year. Sarah's gardeners created a cascade and tree-planted islands, and the pink waterlilies in the pools came to be her pride.

Notre-Dame de Belle-Île delighted in her island, and her island came to delight in her. One day, it is said, when she stopped her carriage in the street in Sauzon, a small boy cried out: 'So that's Sarah Bernhardt! How ugly she is!' Sarah took a gold coin from her pocket and gave it to him. 'That's for you, for telling me the truth.' She had gained yet another admirer.

Sarah Bernhardt in *La Tosca*, OPPOSITE from a photograph, and RIGHT and OVERLEAF as seen by an English cartoonist, 1888. The play was written for her by Sardou, and was first produced in 1887. The amount of electricity generated by one scene was enough, so someone said, to light the streets of London.

SARAH
BERNHARDT
IN THE
FOURTH ACT

In the autumn of 1887, Sarah's rest at Belle-Île was brief. On 24
November she appeared opposite Pierre Berton in a new play which
Sardou had written for her: *La Tosca*. The amount of electricity
generated by one scene of this play would have been enough, so someone observed, to light the streets of London. Pierre Louÿs, the future
novelist and poet, was then a susceptible *collégien*, vainly seeking a god-
dess whom he might worship. Early in the new year he saw Sarah in
La Tosca, and he was overwhelmed by his first passion. Two months
later, still afire with adoration, he waited by Sarah's carriage to see
her leave the Odéon where she had been rehearsing *L'Aveu*.

I waited a long while. Little by little, having seen Sarah Bernhardt's famous
monogram on the horses' harness, the crowd began to collect. At last Sarah
arrived, all fresh in a flowing cloak of embossed velvet, with a black veil
round her head. A little ragamuffin snuggled up to her and asked for a sou.
She put on her coaxing voice, 'Darling . . . let me pass.' And slipped into the

'The one and only Sarah,' again as La Tosca.
From a photograph by Downey.

depths of her carriage, saying to Marquet: 'I'll see you this evening. Don't forget!'

How lucky those people are!

Sarah's first play, *L'Aveu*, was first performed on 27 March 1888. It is a short and cogent melodrama played round the bedside of a dying child. When the mother feels that the child is lost, she confesses to her husband that it is not his, and that the real father is waiting in the next room for news. There is a violent quarrel between the two men, and then the baby dies and the quarrel ends.

For all Sarah's acting *L'Aveu* was poorly received, and it was performed a mere dozen times that year. But it was not to be her only literary venture. She wrote a five-act drama, set in modern Florence: *La Duchesse Catherine* (it was never performed). She wrote a new and vastly successful version of *Adrienne Lecouvreur*. Her *Christmas Story* appeared in *The Silver Fairy Book* in 1895. She turned to the novel, too; and in *Petite Idole*, that strange amalgam of fact and fiction, she was to project herself as Espérance Darbois, the child actress who died on stage at the Théâtre-Français.

At the end of March 1888, suddenly exhausted by the strain of endless tours, of perpetual playing, of personal unhappiness, Sarah was forced to interrupt performances of *La Tosca*. But she did not rest for long. After several weeks she had recovered enough to take the play on tour in the French provinces. In July she went to London, where she played La Tosca with such terrifying effect that men had to leave the theatre in mid performance.

It was on her return that an event of profound domestic importance occurred: the marriage of Maurice. At the age of twenty-three he married a Polish princess, Terka Jablonovska, and left the avenue de Villiers. Maurice was the real great love of Sarah's life, and he was her only lasting passion. To Maurice, a prince's son, who was as handsome as a prince, Sarah had given all the devotion that she had not been able to give to Damala and her lovers, all the affection that her family had not deserved. The shoes he had worn as a child had been with her on her prodigious tours of America; she wore his portrait, a lock of his hair, in a gold locket at her neck. His frequent duels, his indolence, his complete dependence on her – all were forgiven him to the end of her life. Now for the first time he left her roof; and fond though Sarah was of Terka, warmly though she approved of the marriage, there remained a void in her existence.

A dramatic moment in *La Tosca*,
photographed by Nadar in 1887.

There was some consolation. She spent August with Maurice and Terka at Belle-Île. Then, refreshed by the air of Brittany, she set out on yet another tour. She went to the Low Countries, Vienna, Budapest and Bucharest. From Italy she went to Egypt; and Lord Cromer told his nephew, Maurice Baring, that an Egyptian dignitary who had seen *La Tosca* declared: '*C'est chose!*' – a phrase which was used to express something catastrophic. From Cairo Sarah went on to Alexandria, Constantinople, St Petersburg. She returned home by way of Sweden and Norway. And back in Paris in March 1889 she received news of Damala. He begged her to come and see him.

She hastened to him, found him in a little *entresol* at the back of a courtyard in the rue d'Antin. The small dark rooms were sparsely furnished; their only ornaments were the sabre he had worn in *Les Mères ennemies*, a gold crown and a Greek flag. Damala was now taking cocaine as well as morphine; he stayed in bed most of the day, watching his mind grow increasingly unbalanced. Sarah was filled with maternal pity. She had him taken to hospital. On 18 August 1890, at the age of thirty-four, he died.

He was buried in Athens. But visitors to Sarah's *hôtel* always noticed in a place of honour a marble figure that she had sculpted: 'Damala lying on his back with his hands under his handsome head.' She kept the greatest affection for his family and for his memory.

On 23 October 1890, her forty-sixth birthday, Sarah performed in *Cléo-pâtre*, the fourth play that Sardou had written for her. 'What charm, what magic!' cried Anatole France. Maurice Baring was to try to ana-lyse her genius.

No such movement and gestures [so he wrote], no such plastic rhythm, have been seen on the stage since then until Lady Diana Manners as the Madonna in Reinhardt's *Miracle*. . . .

Then there was her voice. . . .

She could express anything, from the fury of the whirlwind to the sigh of a sleepy stream. As she poured out a cup of coffee in one play she said: '*Du sucre, deux morceaux?*' and all the charm of all the Muses seemed to be flower-ing in the four words of that banal breakfast question. When as Cleopatra she approached Antony, saying, '*Je suis la reine d'Egypte*,' one said to oneself: 'Poor Antony!' The fate of Empires, the dominion of the world, the lordship of Rome, will have small chance in the balance against five silver words and a smile; and we thought the world well lost; and we envied Antony and his ruin and his doom.

131

Sarah Bernhardt with Maurice: her son by Henri, Prince de Ligne.

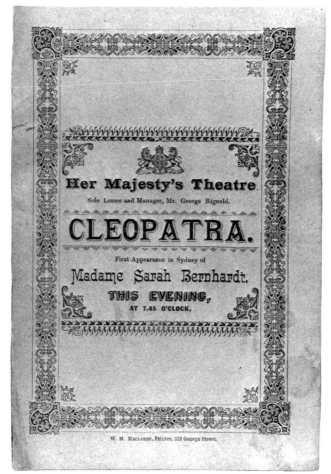

This programme announces Sarah Bernhardt's appearance
as Cleopatra at Her Majesty's Theatre, Sydney.

Sarah, that nineteenth-century Cleopatra, played the Queen of
Egypt until the beginning of January 1891. On 23 January she was
to embark on the most prodigious tour of her career. A few days before
her departure Jules Huret, the journalist, called on her at her new,
delightful and distracting sanctum, 56, boulevard Péreire.

In the bewildering confusion of Oriental and modern, he managed
to note, to his credit, that the walls were hung with Turkey-red cotton
and adorned by Mexican sombreros, feather parasols, and trophies of
lances and daggers. Swarms of Buddhas were scattered about on settees,

132

SARAH BERNHARDT
"CLEOPATRA."

Falk

COPYRIGHT
1891.

496 GEORGE STREET.
SYDNEY

Sarah Bernhardt as Cleopatra: a photograph taken
in Australia.

with Japanese monsters, Chinese curios, ivory-work and bronzes. The
floor was covered with Oriental carpets thickly strewn with skins, and
jackals' and hyenas' heads and panthers' paws met him at every step.
Sarah received him in her study, wearing an ample cream cashmere
peignoir trimmed with lace. He asked her the extent of her tour; and,
accustomed to journalists, she handed him the answer in writing. Huret
was astounded. 'Don't you feel sorry to think of leaving Paris for two
years?' 'Not at all,' replied Sarah. 'Far from it. It is just the same as
going to the Bois de Boulogne.... I love travelling.' On 23 January

133

OVERLEAF A delightful and distracting Parisian sanctum: a corner of
Sarah Bernhardt's *hôtel*, 56, boulevard Péreire.

she left according to schedule; in September 1893, after thirty-two months, she ended her odyssey at Lisbon with a profit of three and a half million francs.

It was at this moment of wealth that she became the manager of the Théâtre de la Renaissance. She managed the theatre for five years, until 1898. During those years, among many revivals, she produced twelve new plays. Two of them, *Izeyl* by Eugène Morand and Armand Silvestre, and *Lorenzaccio* by Alfred de Musset, had little more than seventy performances. Only one, *Gismonda*, reached its hundredth performance. But if the Renaissance was not a happy school for dramatists, it was a brilliant nursery for actors. Sarah set three new actors at the head of her company. One of them, Abel Deval, was excellent; the others, Lucien Guitry and de Max, were outstanding. Lucien Guitry was thirty-three; but having spent nine years acting in St Petersburg, he had not yet established himself in Paris. Under Sarah's management he rose to eminence. Édouard de Max was only twenty-four when she took the Renaissance; and it was Sarah herself who launched this admirable actor, her own ideal partner: indeed her best partner after Mounet-Sully. De Max was regally handsome, the incarnation of the prince of legend.

Early in 1894, with Guitry and de Max, Sarah appeared in *Izeyl*, a somewhat colourless drama set in India six centuries before Christ. It ran for a mere two months, after which she briefly revived *Fédora* and closed the theatre. Then, invisible for flowers, accompanied by her usual phenomenal pile of luggage and a black page to spray her compartment with verbena and mount guard outside her rooms at the Savoy, she left for London.

It seemed that Sarah, like Cleopatra, was not condemned by the years. And yet she was sometimes sad. Her perpetual activity, her manifold triumphs, her defiant motto *Quand même* were essential to her existence; but they grew increasingly difficult to maintain. And, so far as the Press were concerned, the days of unqualified praise were already ending. 'This Sarah the Younger is a fascinating, seductive, supple and sinuous creature, with the smile of a Sphinx and the voice of a Siren,' decided the critic William Archer, watching her in *Izeyl* at Daly's Theatre. 'But ah! You should have seen her mother, twenty years ago! The daughter imitates her marvellously; but the copy is mechanical, and sometimes a little coarse.'

136

Sarah Bernhardt as Medea.

Sarah Bernhardt as Marguerite Gautier in *La Dame aux camélias*, 1879.
From a photograph by Falk.

And in *Phèdre*, too, he felt that Sarah was not at her best. 'In the more violent passages the sense of strain becomes painful and almost intolerable, Mme Bernhardt seems to grind out her voice through her clenched teeth, and, moreover, to froth up her voice as they froth up eggs or chocolate. There was rather too much of this effect on Friday evening: "*C'est Vénus-a tout entière à sa proie attachée-a. . . .*" But in the languishing passages she was nothing less than divine.' Divine indeed; and the theatre rocked with the plaudits of the young, and the curtain slid up and down, up and down, in response to their thunders, like the guillotine blade on a busy morning.

It was about now that the divinity was interviewed in *The Strand Magazine*. She told the reporter how she studied the intellectual composition of her rôle, read every criticism of the character, every memoir and biography of the period; she told him how, on stage, she was sometimes exalted by the situation, fired by some personal remembrance. She told him of the wardrobe said to surpass the wardrobe of Queen Elizabeth, the wardrobe worth half a million francs which she kept at the boulevard Péreire. She told him how she designed the fabrics of her dresses, refused to have cheap theatrical tinsel, insisted on hand embroideries in gold thread and silk. 'What *is* best always looks best.' It had, none the less, to fulfil the needs of the theatre. On one occasion, in London, she needed a piece of stuff to make a peplum which she could wear in *Phèdre*; a woman admirer searched London, and brought back something which looked like a silver dream. Sarah gave one glance and said that it would look flat in the footlights, which was true.

She dressed with extraordinary and seductive art. Reynaldo Hahn noticed a white muslin dress which she wore in *La Dame aux camélias*. It moulded her unique figure, the figure which had created a new kind of feminine grace. And, watching her in London in the ball scene in *Lysiane*, Hahn recorded her pale blue dress, low cut, with a little lace on the corsage and some flowers. It was one of those dresses which Sarah had made, those dresses which had helped to make Sarah. They had established her type, a type of woman unknown before her, a type which countless women had since wanted to become. Even in her everyday clothes Sarah kept the same cut. She liked a draped corsage and a skirt which was tighter at the ankles than the hips and seemed to turn in a spiral around her. The spiral had always been Sarah's linear formula. In all her gestures, reflected Hahn, one rediscovered a spiral principle.

The author of *L'Aiglon* and *La Princesse lointaine*:
Edmond Rostand (1868–1918).

On 5 January 1895, in the great courtyard of the École militaire, Sarah Bernhardt watched the degradation of Captain Dreyfus, a Jewish officer in the French army. He had been convicted of sending confidential military documents to the German military attaché. Anti-German feeling ran high; anti-semitism has always run strong in the French nature. Sarah was moved by Dreyfus' impassiveness, and she could not believe in his guilt. In 1898, with the publication of 'J'accuse . . .', Emile Zola's open letter to the President of the Republic, the Dreyfus affair was to enter its phase of acute controversy. Five Ministers of War and three successive Prime Ministers were forced to resign. Families were divided, friendships were endangered. Lemaître and Coppée, Maurice Bernhardt himself, sided against Dreyfus; Sardou and Sarah remained convinced of his innocence. Sarah's support of Dreyfus led Maurice to leave Paris in fury, without even warning his mother or bidding her goodbye. Not until the suicide of Colonel Henry, who had falsified the evidence against Dreyfus, and the revelation of Dreyfus' innocence, did he return repentant and convinced. The Dreyfus affair was not mentioned again in Sarah's presence. It was the only cause of dissension that would ever divide her and her son. Sarah could be unjust and arbitrary, unbearable, contradictory, provocative, rebellious and intransigent. She could not be mean. Her friends long remembered how boldly she proclaimed her belief in Dreyfus and (in spite of her intimates) how passionately she defended him.

Not long before the degradation of Dreyfus, a young poet, Edmond Rostand, had presented himself at 56, boulevard Péreire. He was to write some of Sarah's most conspicious triumphs, and she was to give him his celebrity. On 5 April 1895, supported by Guitry and de Max, Sarah launched *La Princesse lointaine*. 'It may not make a sou,' she had said, 'but I don't care. I think it is superb. No artist could fail to stage it.'

La Princesse lointaine depended on Sarah's power of creating unearthly beauty, of realizing a dream. The first act described Mélissinde, Princess Far Away, a being of irresistible fascination and supernatural loveliness. In the second act she appeared, and fulfilled imagination. The verse was graceful though unremarkable; then, suddenly, there emerged a lyric which was strangely and hauntingly musical. Geoffrey Rudel, the troubadour prince, recited it in the first act; in the second act the Rhyme of Princess Far Away was spoken by Sarah Bernhardt herself. Everyone waited for that moment. At last the moment came.

MADAME SARAH BERNHARDT.
AS PRINCESSE LOINTAINE.

Sarah Bernhardt in the title-rôle of *La Princesse lointaine.*
She launched the play in 1895.

Car c'est chose suprême
D'aimer sans qu'on vous aime,
D'aimer toujours, quand même,
    Sans cesse,
D'une amour incertaine,
Plus noble d'être vaine...
Et j'aime la lointaine
    Princesse.

Car c'est chose divine
D'aimer quand on devine,
Rêve, invente, imagine
    À peine...
Le seul rêve intéresse,
Vivre sans rêve, qu'est-ce?
Et j'aime la Princesse
    Lointaine!

The indifferent poetry of *La Princesse lointaine* turned, as Sarah spoke it, to gold; but her greatest triumph was a triumph of grace, and even Sarcey applauded the final vision of Mélissinde arriving, like Cleopatra in her barge, decked in her finest raiment and followed by a gorgeous retinue, to take the veil. Maurice Rostand, Edmond's son, was in time to wear the ring which Mélissinde wore in the last act of the play. It was a sapphire ring set by Lalique in the purest Sarah Bernhardt style.

La Princesse lointaine was magnificently cast, spectacularly beautiful; but, as Sarah had feared, it was not popular. It had cost her more than 200,000 francs, and it ran for thirty-one performances. Despondently she revived *La Dame aux camélias*.

It was about now that Edmond Rostand took his son to see her for the first time. At the age of five, Maurice Rostand was led into her dressing-room at the Théâtre de la Renaissance. Sarah was never too solemn or too grand to put herself in a child's place. She had an instinctive sympathy with childhood. Maurice Rostand saw her at her dressing-table, making herself up for the first act of the play. She seemed to him both incredibly old and incredibly young. There was a bevy of lady's maids scurrying around her, and she was growing impatient with them. But even these scenes had something theatrical about them, and one wanted to applaud at the end. The outbursts were all the less alarming since Sarah often ended by distributing some of her large stock of stage jewels to her servants.

SARAH BERNHARDT

On that distant day which I now recall [wrote Maurice Rostand], I went into that eternal dressing-room which I was hardly ever to leave again. When Sarah saw me she stopped for a moment dabbing a brilliant rouge on her cheeks (which she was doing in a frenzy), and, in that voice which will never be anyone's but hers, despite her imitators, that voice in which there was everything, artifice and sincerity, genius and even an English accent, that same voice with which she spoke to the high priest in *Athalie* and to a little spectator of five years old who came to see her, she ordered a kind of personage, ill-shaven and dressed in black, to have a spectacular tea prepared at once for me, and to serve it here. It was a matter of cream-puffs and *tisane Saint-Marceaux*, because, for Sarah, even children were obliged to taste champagne.

The black personage was Pitou, her personal and permanent secretary, a strange silhouette out of a novel. . . . The tea was prepared, and then came the performance which I was trembling to see because it was the first time that I was going to see Sarah Bernhardt. . . .

I watched the performance from the director's stage-box, where my father had taken me with my nurse. Suddenly, in the last act, when Marguerite Gautier, about to die, looks out of the window and thinks she sees something outside, Sarah looked as if she suddenly saw me. And, transforming the text, she began to talk about little Maurice, whom she recognized in the stage-box.

I don't know why, I burst into tears. Had Sarah wanted to show me that afternoon that she was performing specially for me? She had such astonishing intuition that she would have understood that it is not always unworthy of a great tragic actress to perform for a poet of five years old. . . . Oh, wonderful contagion of the theatre! Even if my destiny had not been decided already, it was decided that day. . . .

I was to come away from that matinée with something that I can only compare with sunstroke, and, struck by Sarah's sun, was it not that of a whole generation? . . . There is something mysterious in Sarah's case, which is that her most lasting radiance began precisely when the curtain fell. For her, as for all great people, as for all great works, the word 'end' was a beginning.

Meanwhile, in 1895, Sarah was so tired of her theatre that, for a time, she handed it over to Guitry. She had spent a fortune; she was constantly spending a fortune: on Belle-Île (which had cost her nearly 700,000 francs); on her household with its numerous servants, its three or four carriages and six horses (among them the fairytale carriage, with its two chestnut horses, in which she would drive through Paris, muffled up in chinchilla, even in July). Sarah was spending a fortune, too, on the ten to twenty guests (and they ate well) who arrived for nearly every meal. It was time to make a fortune again. She prepared to return once more to America; this time she would go for ten months.

Maurice Rostand (1891–1968), dramatist, and son of Edmond Rostand.
From a photograph taken in about 1923.

'It sometimes seems', wrote William Archer, sadly, 'as though Sarah Bernhardt were no longer a real woman, but an exquisitely contrived automaton. ... There is a noble simplicity, a searching directness, in the art of Eleonora Duse which comes as a relief after the excessive artifice of Sarah's later manner. One has a sensation of passing out into the fresh air from an alcove redolent of patchouli.'

May Agate remarks that in France la Duse was never considered remotely the equal of Sarah Bernhardt. The idea of rivalry seemed to have been confined solely to the English-speaking world. Sarah herself considered la Duse much inferior to Réjane. 'Eleonora Duse', she wrote, 'is an actress rather than an artist; she walks in the paths laid down by others. She certainly does not imitate them, for she plants flowers where there were trees, and trees where there were flowers. But she has not made a personage rise up from her art, a personage identified with her name; she has not created a being, a vision which calls forth her memory.' Of her many colleagues, Sarah most admired Mounet-Sully, as he had been in her early days, and later Lucien Guitry and Gabrielle Réjane. Irving, she said, was far from a great actor, but perhaps the greatest artist in the world.

As for her own later manner, William Archer lamented that the gold of Sarah's genius had, alas, been transmuted into cast-iron; and there was a certain truth in his criticism. French audiences, claimed May Agate, would only go and see Sarah in flamboyant, rather tawdry plays. French theatrical taste, insisted Miss Agate, had been 'wilfully retarded' by Sarcey, who influenced public opinion well into the 1890s; and Sarcey turned his back upon *les abominations russes et scandinaves* and finally rejected even Shakespeare. Sarah learned from experience that neither the classics nor modern realism ever drew audiences to her theatre for long.

Whatever the reason, her partnership with Sardou was producing a monotonous series of melodramas, all impossible without her, all devised to show off her dramatic points. *Gismonda*, for example, was luxuriously set in fifteenth-century Athens. But Sarah and Sardou had accustomed the public to short, sharp shocks and protracted agonies; and now, instead of dying impressively in the fifth act, Sarah married Lucien Guitry. 'And that is a very good idea, too,' considered Jules Lemaître. 'For no doubt a play that had two hundred performances with an unhappy ending would have three or four hundred with a happy one.' Lemaître was wrong. *Gismonda* ran for a mere one hundred

Sarah Bernhardt in *Leah*. From a photograph by Downey.

and three performances. Paris missed the customary agony. When, in 1895, Sarah played *Gismonda* in London, Archer confessed to 'a growing distaste for this bogus history and Brummagem archaeology of Monsieur Sardou's,' for these one-part plays filled out with cardboard figures. 'Someone to cajole and someone to murder are', so he snapped, 'the two necessities of artistic existence for Mme Sarah Bernhardt; and the Eminent Academician is her most active purveyor of victims.'

When Sarah turned, in this London summer of 1895, from Sardou to Rostand, and appeared in *La Princesse lointaine*, a softened Archer declared that she chanted the part of Mélissinde to perfection; but the critic of *The Sketch* became so weary of the exploited golden voice that he 'grew a leaning towards the heresy of bimetallism in voices'. George Bernard Shaw, relentless, came out of Daly's Theatre convinced that 'M. Rostand's Princess Far Away will die of Mélissinde.'

Such criticism seemed ineffectual. Early in October Sarah was touring in France and Belgium; and in Brussels, one morning, there was a battle of flowers. 'I remember', recalls a spectator in the avenue Louise, 'that blue was the dominant colour that season. I had just told my hostess that if Sarah should join the battle, she would have blue flowers; and sure enough there she came in a victoria, completely covered in blue cornflowers, wrapped in delightful greyish furs and rugs, and to deafening applause, bowing like a queen.'

It was the queen of actresses who left Le Havre on 3 January 1896 for another tour of the United States. She made a royal progress through America. She received deputations from several cities where she could not play. In one they would have erected triumphal arches for her; in another they wanted to illuminate the town.

Late in July she returned to France; late in September she returned to the Théâtre de la Renaissance in *La Dame aux camélias*, a revival even more successful than usual, for, instead of playing it in modern dress, she staged it in the costume of its period. A week after her return, this triumph was briefly interrupted to let her appear at Versailles before the Tsar; for Nicholas II, asked by the French Ambassador what entertainment he chose for his official visit, had answered in two words: 'Sarah Bernhardt.'

In December she took the title-role in the first performance of Musset's *Lorenzaccio*, and received a vigorous welcome from the critics. 'She was', cried Catulle Mendès, 'from beginning to end, and at every

Sarah in the title-rôle of Alfred de Musset's *Lorenzaccio*. She performed the part in 1896, at the age of fifty-two, and Catulle Mendès declared that she was 'from beginning to end, and at every moment, incomparably sublime'. In fact the play was one of her least successful productions at the Théâtre de la Renaissance.

Sarah Bernhardt, from a photograph taken
by Histed of London in about 1903.

moment, incomparably sublime. And the fête that Paris is preparing for her will express all the gratitude of a century and of a nation.' It was, in fact, a week after the opening of *Lorenzaccio* that the official glorification of Sarah took place in Paris. Henry Bauer, the journalist, organized *la Journée Sarah Bernhardt*.

Not since the various glorifications accorded to Victor Hugo had there been such a national event.

On the morning of 9 December 1896, the elect assembled for a banquet in honour of Sarah Bernhardt. They were never to forget the emotion and applause as she made her entrance. Nobody ever moved better than Sarah. Jules Renard, the novelist, seeing her come down a spiral staircase, said that the staircase seemed to turn, and she to be motionless. Today she came down the stairs to the banqueting room, the huge Salle du Zodiaque, in the Grand Hotel, rue Scribe. They acclaimed her wildly.

The long train of her beautiful white dress, trimmed with English lace, embroidered with gold, and bordered with chinchilla, followed her like a graceful tame serpent down the stairs. At every turn in the staircase she bent over the railing and twined her arm like an ivy-wreath round the velvet pillars while she acknowledged the acclamations with her disengaged hand. Her lithe and slender body scarcely seemed to touch the earth. She was wafted towards us in a halo of glory.

After the compliments and embraces she took her place at the table of honour on the dais under a canopy of green velvet. Her delicate profile, the profile of a princess in legend, stood out against a tapestry which gracefully represented 'Time in chains'. On her right sat Victorien Sardou, on her left Henry Bauer. There were five hundred guests, all famous in science, politics and business, in literature and in the arts, in society and in the theatre. There were three kinds of menu, each designed by a different artist. Among the dishes were *gâteaux Sarah* and *bombe Tosca*. After the banquet, Sardou proposed a toast to 'the great and good Sarah'. The Colonne choir (accompanied by the Colonne orchestra) sang a cantata composed to her greater glory. Then Sarah made her regal departure. 'As she went slowly up the winding stair, from time to time sending a smile or a wave of her hand to her admirers below, she seemed almost to be mounting in triumph towards the sky.'

And then the assembly followed her to the Théâtre de la Renaissance.

Here, as in the rue Scribe, mounted soldiers were keeping back the crowds. And in they went: the privileged who had paid a fortune for their seats; the critics who, for once, had discarded criticism; the deputations from the students' associations, from the École Polytechnique, the Conservatoire, the École des Beaux-Arts; the non-commissioned officers of the Paris garrison.

Sarah performed the second act of *Phèdre* and the fourth act of *Rome vaincue*. Then the curtain rose to show her robed in white and gold and seated on a throne of flowers under a canopy of green palms, camellias and orchids. Women in peplums, crowned with roses, posed in adoring attitudes about her. Then a young student paid homage to the eternal youth of the artist. And then, in turn, the poets Francois Coppée, Catulle Mendès, André Theuriet, Edmond Haraucourt, José Maria de Heredia and Edmond Rostand read their sonnets in praise of Sarah Bernhardt. When the curtain fell on this apotheosis there was tumult: shouts, cheers, applause, the stamping of feet. Women tore flowers from their hair and from their corsages to throw them on the stage.

Small wonder that Sarah took it for granted that she was the greatest actress in the world, just as Queen Victoria took it for granted that she was Queen of England.

Sarah Bernhardt in everyday dress. From a photograph by Sarony.

4
A Great Institution

Sarah Bernhardt as Sainte-Thérèse in *La Vierge d'Avila*,
by Catulle Mendès. She first produced the play in 1906.

HALF A CENTURY BEFORE, Rachel had magnificently played the part of Pauline, the Christian convert in *Polyeucte*. At Easter 1897, Sarah Bernhardt, who was also Jewish, again moved Paris by religious fervour in the first performance of *La Samaritaine* by Edmond Rostand.

Jesus asks Photine to give Him water [Sarcey explained]. She refuses to dip her pitcher. Then He speaks to her of another thirst by which she is devoured, unknowing: a thirst that He alone can assuage. For He possesses the water of truth. He is the Messiah. Photine, moved, charmed, overwhelmed, in ecstasy, listens to him; and Sarah must be heard as, transfigured, drinking in the words of life, she repeats that single word with the ardour of a neophyte: '*J'écoute! J'écoute!*' It is she who fills the second act. Burning with fire divine, she hastens to evangelize the people. . . . The Samaritan woman triumphs. The courtesans weep and confess their sins, matrons cast away their jewels, men weep. No, you cannot imagine the picture unless you have seen it. . . .

All the religious fervour which had possessed Sarah as a child, at the convent of Grand-Champs, seemed to come upon her now; and Rostand dedicated his play 'to Madame Sarah Bernhardt who was a flame and a prayer'.

Reynaldo Hahn long remembered Sarah as Photine, wearing her blue and yellow robes, their folds so complex yet so simple, one of those costumes which only Sarah wore. Her hands were heavy with rings, her feet were bare. One felt that this Samaritan woman, this creature of pleasure, was drenched with perfumes. Hahn also recalled how, after the first act, Sarah swiftly rose to her feet; someone threw a shawl round her shoulders. She went back to her dressing-room, asked for her part, and, with unheard-of speed, recited the hundreds of lines of the second act, taking all her cues, while a score of people came in and out. Sometimes she broke off to give an order, or rebuke the prompter, or to hold out her hand to a new arrival. . . .

Soon after *La Samaritaine*, it was announced that Eleonora Duse would perform in Paris that summer; indeed, her impresario was already negotiating with various theatres. Sarah promptly offered her the Renaissance free of charge, and a contract was signed for ten performances in June, to alternate with her own.

In May, when la Duse published the list of plays she would perform, there was stupefaction. Most astonishing, she had chosen to make her

'There is a noble simplicity in the art of Eleonora Duse which certainly comes as a relief after the excessive artifice of Sarah's later manner.' So wrote the English critic William Archer. Sarah's great contemporary is seen here in *La Città morta* by d'Annunzio.

début in Sarah's theatre in *La Dame aux camélias*. Sarah did not object to this provocative choice, but the Press commented on it severely. The choice, so they said, had been made by Gabriele d'Annunzio, with whom la Duse had just begun her liaison: d'Annunzio, who had not yet seen Sarah Bernhardt on the stage.

The early summer brought a battle that recalled the conflict of forty years ago between Rachel and la Ristori. Again an Italian actress came to Paris, again the audience were to watch a theatrical contest. Sarah was fifty-two, resplendent with her international triumphs; la Duse was thirty-eight, her reputation was not comparable, but she had the advantage of her years, the advantage of novelty, and the greater advantage of pleasing Sarah's detractors. La Duse enjoyed a considerable success, largely due to curiosity, but the comparison which she had sought was hardly made. There was no comparison to make.

On 14 June there was an extraordinary performance in aid of the fund for a statue to Dumas *fils*. Two Dumas plays were chosen. La Duse performed the second act of *La Femme de Claude*, and Sarah the fourth and fifth of *La Dame aux camélias*. The receipts were colossal (31,000 francs); and it was the only time that the two actresses appeared in the same programme. This crucial performance was witnessed by d'Annunzio himself.

D'Annunzio, despite his liaison, did not conceal his preference for Sarah. '*Belle! Magnifique! D'Annunzienne!*' he cried when he first met her. Eleonora, he felt, was sincere, but Sarah was poetic. Romain Rolland shared his preference and wrote caustically that la Duse 'was even further from genius than Sarah'.

It was said that the personality of Eleonora Duse sometimes impeded her portrayal, but that Sarah's always illuminated hers. La Duse so sublimated the part of Marguerite Gautier that she could play it with woollen spencers ill-concealed beneath her négligées. The approach was intellectual, and as far removed from reality as it could be. In the summer of 1894, in London, Sarah herself had seen la Duse as Marguerite Gautier. 'Signora Duse's conception', she told a reporter, 'strikes me as being absolutely original, and, if I may say so, particularly Italian, but I do not think we differ much as to essentials.' In time she came to be less benevolent; and she published such harsh judgment of la Duse that the Italian actress replied: 'Tell Mme Bernhardt that I am not writing my memoirs, nor have I any intention of writing them; but she had better pray God I never change my mind.'

Sarah Bernhardt's complexion, wrote George Bernard
Shaw, 'showed that she had not studied modern art
in vain'. It inspired Jules Chéret with this poster
for rice-powder in 1890.

On 17 June 1897, when la Duse had finished in Paris, Sarah opened
her new London season. It was indeed her season, not that of the dramatists she represented, and *The Times* simply headed its article 'Mme
Sarah Bernhardt at the Adelphi.'

Yet, for all her fame, there were cynics who now compared her to
an alarm clock, going off at intervals with subdued ticking between the
paroxysms; and whatever her supremacy over la Duse, one begins to
ask if Sarah merely chose the wrong parts, if she were growing stale,
or if her powers were failing.

But Sarah was not competing with la Duse alone; she was also chal-
lenged by an actress whom she loved and admired, an actress eleven
years younger than herself. In London, in that Jubilee month of 1897,

in Maurice Donnay's *La Douloureuse*, Réjane was earning the heartfelt applause of London.

And there was, that summer, one performance in London with which none could compete. Sarah herself must have realized this as she arrived at dawn at the Glenesks' house in Piccadilly to watch the Diamond Jubilee procession. 'Wonderfullest sight I ever saw,' wrote Sarah's fellow-guest, Ellen Terry. 'All was perfect, but the little Queen herself more dignified than the whole procession put together.'

October 1897 found Sarah performing in Belgium. She returned to France to produce a series of unfortunate plays. By the end of 1898, pursued by an inexorable series of failures, she was convinced that an evil spell had been cast on the Théâtre de la Renaissance. She put up her lease for sale and bade farewell with *La Dame aux camélias* in November and December. Then she signed a twenty-five-year lease, beginning on 1 January 1899, for the Théâtre des Nations near the banks of the Seine; a theatre which, characteristically enough, she re-named the Théâtre Sarah-Bernhardt.

Sarah's new theatre was a much more sensible enterprise than its predecessor. The Renaissance had 900 seats, the Sarah-Bernhardt had 1700. *Gismonda* cost 32,000 francs a week at the Renaissance, and if the house was full every night the weekly profit could not exceed 16,000; the same play, produced at the Sarah-Bernhardt, might cost 40,000 francs; but if, for a week, it drew the maximum receipts, the profits might be 55,000.

It was in this theatre that on 20 May 1899 Sarah gave her first performance as Hamlet. Long before her appearance, rumour said, she had adapted herself to the part by wearing Hamlet's costume in the boulevard Péreire; and 'it was an amusement of a very piquant character to hear the Prince of Denmark alluding during breakfast to the latest incidents of Parisian life.' Now, when she appeared on stage, she recalled to some the Hamlet of Delacroix. The translated *Hamlet* was – at least to Parisian ears – an immense success; and Maurice Baring declared that it was Sarah's performance which first gave the French public an exact idea of *Hamlet*. Her characterization was strikingly original, and roused such heated comments that Catulle Mendès fought a duel with an opposing critic, Georges Vanor, over the colour of Hamlet's hair – or Sarah's hair, which was the same thing, that season. Mounet-Sully went ten times to study Sarah's performance; and, when

Hamlet, Princess of Denmark. A photograph of Sarah Bernhardt
in the part which she first performed in 1899.

the curtain fell, Hernani and Doña Sol, Ruy Blas and the Queen of Spain would discuss interpretations until the small hours of the morning. In June, to allow the contractors to work on her theatre, Sarah went to play *Hamlet* in London.

And so, on 12 June 1899, at the Adelphi Theatre, London witnessed one of the most remarkable performances in the annals of Shakespearean production. 'You are so lucky in England,' Sarah was to tell an English journalist. 'You have Shakespeare. You can never quite forget him.' She spoke, perhaps, more truly than she understood. It was an audacious venture to interpret the most controversial character in English drama during the reign of Henry Irving; and it was doubly audacious, for the young Prince of Denmark was not only to be played by a woman, and by a Frenchwoman at that, but by a woman fifty-four years of age.

As a *tour de force* Mme Bernhardt's Hamlet was bound to be interesting [reported *The Times*]. As a *succès de curiosité* it was bound to attract the town. But it is much more than this that Mme Sarah Bernhardt has to offer. Her Hamlet is a rendering worked out with care and intelligence and with a consistent grip upon the character as the actress conceives it.... No one who is an admirer of Mme Bernhardt's wonderful art and wonderful personality will come away disappointed.

There were times when Sarah's acting was inspired by long years of practice, or by technical precision. There were also times when, as she used to say, the god descended. Desmond MacCarthy remembered a moment in Sarah's *Hamlet* when Hamlet ran his sword through the arras and heard the body fall. He hoped that he had killed the king. Sarah stood still for a moment, 'tiptoe, like a great black exclamation mark – her sword glittering above her head.' It was one of those moments which entitled her to say: '*Le dieu est venu ce soir.*'

Opinions, however, were not entirely golden. *Punch* was quick to suggest that Irving should play Ophelia. Max Beerbohm made the neatest comment in an article called 'Hamlet, Princess of Denmark'. The only compliment, he said, 'one can conscientiously pay her is that her Hamlet was, from first to last, *très grande dame*'.

She was now, above all, *très grande dame*. Let us look at her, in her mid-fifties, through the eyes of an English critic, J. T. Grein.

When she is at her best she can save any cause, even the most hopeless.... True, the autumn of her life has alloyed base metal with the pure gold of her

162

The divinity at home: Sarah Bernhardt with a granddaughter, and a faithful attendant.

Sarah Bernhardt as Marie-Antoinette in *Varennes*, by Henri Lavedan.

voice; it is less tender, less bewitching than it was; but her other powers have increased. Her method is no longer impulsive, or, rather, explosive as I would like to call it. Nor does she at times sink into periods of apathy as formerly. She is more even now. The fervour of her passion has lost none of its intensity, but it grows more gradually, and when the climax comes – those wonderful moments when her whole being is ablaze, when she is entirely lost as it were in her assumed character – it strikes home with peerless force. She has reached, I venture to say, the zenith of her career, for she has done with star-acting and episodical bravura; she has become a harmonious part of the picture, and that is, as I contend, the very essential of great acting.

There had been a time when Sarah enjoyed astonishing the world. She was not the only star to recognize the value of publicity; she had simply publicized herself better than most. She had created a legend for the public. Now, however, she had done with fostering absurdities. To her pupil, May Agate (James's sister), she represented 'the perfection of taste and good manners. We knew her as a devoted mother and grandmother.' Sarah advised Mrs Agate that if she could not tour with May herself, she should engage a reliable chaperone, '*par exemple, la veuve d'un clergyman*'. Sarah was more mellow now, more punctilious, as if she felt that she were an ambassador from France. Yvonne Lanco, as a small child, used to see Sarah Bernhardt pass in her carriage. A Negro servant in scarlet livery sat beside the groom. But Sarah herself, always dressed in white, did not seem like Sarah Barnum. She seemed to the child a very great lady.

It was this very great lady who, in September 1899, returned to Paris to supervise the decoration of her theatre. Parisian theatres had always been furnished in red. Sarah's auditorium was draped from ceiling to floor in buttercup yellow velvet framed in ivory white.

The stage, instead of being inclined, is horizontal [explained *The Sketch*] because the artist thinks it absurd that the persons at the back should be made to look taller than those in the first plan; and it has no prompter's box. Also, it is laid in waxed marquetry. To satisfy her taste for hygiene and also for perfumes, Mme Bernhardt has had the auditorium entirely washed over with benjoin. The foyer, the buffet, and the smoking-room are luxuriously furnished, and there is a pharmacy at the command of persons accidentally indisposed.

In the public foyer, which looked out on to the place du Châtelet, ten murals represented Mme Bernhardt, life-size, as Lorenzaccio,

Phèdre, Théodora, la Princesse lointaine, la Tosca, and Gismonda. Mme Bernhardt's 'dressing-room' was not merely a dressing-room, but an extensive apartment of five rooms on two floors. A double door and three steps led from the stage into an ante-room twenty-one feet long and twelve feet wide. Then came a large Empire drawing-room hung with yellow satin and furnished with Empire furniture (an Empire style, it must be confessed, revised by Lalique). Finally came Sarah's dressing-room with a tall dressing-table, wardrobes enough to hold fifty costumes, a monumental washstand, a bathtub and a gigantic three-panelled mirror. These three communicating rooms on the second floor of the theatre overlooked the avenue Victoria. And from the ante-room a narrow stairway led to a ground floor dining-room large enough to seat a dozen guests. To one side were a pantry and a small kitchen. For the next twenty-three years, on first nights, the whole theatrical world would pass in homage through this 'dressing-room', which was famous for its luxury; and every Sunday the elect were invited to dinner.

On 16 December 1899 Sarah re-opened her theatre. A brilliant audience, including President Loubet, admired some revolutions in theatrical design. Next day, on the stage of the Théâtre Sarah-Bernhardt, Edmond Rostand read *L'Aiglon* to her company.

Only a woman supremely sure of her public and her powers would have dared attempt what she attempted now. Thirty-one years before Sarah Bernhardt had entered upon her glory as Zanetto. Now, at fifty-six, she would take the part of another boy: the son of Napoleon. Since the days of Beaumarchais and Chérubin, women have played adolescent boys on the French stage. *Le travesti*, as it is called in France, has been not only permissible but customary. Sarah Bernhardt was made for *le travesti*, for it implies a certain sexlessness. And Sarah, who was so feminine in the rôles which demanded charm, could, if need be, divest herself of her glamour and feline grace, and suggest qualities of mind and spirit.

Rostand's play was designed as a centre-piece for the Paris Exhibition of 1900. It was to be historically perfect. He himself had written the play surrounded by prints and portraits of l'Aiglon. Sarah had even gone with him to visit the Vienna Museum and the apartments at Schönbrunn where l'Aiglon had died. She had brought back a pile of trinkets that bore his likeness to accustom herself to his appearance.

Poet, aesthete and man of letters, and a friend
of Sarah Bernhardt's: Comte Robert de Montesquiou
(1855–1921). From a drypoint by Paul Helleu.

She borrowed the imperial cradle for the final scene from Vienna; she
supervised the footwear of the actors. Long before the performance she
wore men's clothes in order to grow accustomed to them and to forget
her feminine gestures. (She could not, it seems, entirely forget her
femininity: an admirer who gave her his arm found that his sleeve was
scented for days.)

The first night of *L'Aiglon* took place on 15 March 1900. All Paris
had assembled in the Théâtre Sarah-Bernhardt. Maurice Rostand, now
eight years old, sat in a box with his mother for his first first night.
Years afterwards he professed to remember old Sardou, like an elderly
Gavroche, with his white silk scarf; and Jean Lorrain, the Symbolist
poet, with his complexion mottled like galantine, his hands adorned
with ostentatious rings. Robert de Montesquiou, the aesthete and man
of letters, was there, striking the very poses of his portraits.

The first night was a battle – at least it had all the makings of a battle.

167

Sarah Bernhardt as the Duc de Reichstadt in *L'Aiglon*. She first performed the part in 1900, in her fifty-sixth year. OPPOSITE the ageing actress in what proved to be a triumphant play.

The audience were critical. Besides, in 1900 the Dreyfus affair was raging once again, and plays, like everything else, had become a party question. A party of Nationalists was ready to praise or condemn *L'Aiglon*, and a party of Dreyfusards was ready to condemn or praise it. Both parties were swept off their feet. The fact that Sarah was a woman, and a middle-aged woman, was forgotten once she had spoken. L'Aiglon stood before them. When, in the first scene, Sarah spoke the line: '*Je n'aime pas beaucoup que la France soit neutre . . .*' there was a roar of applause. In the scene of the history lesson, Napoleon II gave his schoolmaster an account of the battle of Austerlitz. Sarah played with an increasing *accelerando* and *crescendo*: '*Il suit l'ennemi; sent qu'il l'a dans la main. . . .*' She carried off the lines with a pace and intensity which went through the theatre like an electric shock. People were crying everywhere. When the final curtain fell, there was a rain of violets – the Bonaparte flowers – on the stage. Rostand and Sarah Bernhardt had touched the public heart: had stirred the public pride in Napoleon and his dynasty thirty years after the catastrophe of Sedan.

The triumph of *L'Aiglon* was to continue all through the summer; and Sarah, in her famous carriage with the chestnut horses, often went to visit the Rostands in the house they had taken near Montmorency. Sometimes, to the delight of Maurice Rostand, she would bring her two little granddaughters, Simone and Lysiane; they both looked like Sarah at different periods in her life. Maurice Rostand was long to remember those magic days of childhood when Sarah tossed her chinchilla coat to her favourite greyhound, and proved that her tousled hair was naturally curly by pouring Heidsieck Monopole all over it.

With a break in August so that Sarah could rest, *L'Aiglon* ran for 237 performances. It might have continued until its five-hundredth performance had not Sarah undertaken a new six-months' tour in the United States, from November 1900 to April 1901. It was understood that on her return she would revive *L'Aiglon*, and that in this revival she was determined to have Coquelin as Flambeau.

On Bastille Day 1901, after a season in London, they gave *L'Aiglon* at the Théâtre Sarah-Bernhardt. Coquelin played Flambeau; and the Parisian critics, and Rostand himself, were overwhelmed by his brilliance. Reynaldo Hahn, in admiration, watched Sarah and Coquelin together. 'How Sarah listens to him! How she lets him act! What understanding between them! How well they know the public!' On a visit to Brussels, he saw Sarah as Marguerite Gautier with Coquelin as M.

Madame Sarah playing draughts, probably with her secretary, Pitou.

Sarah Bernhardt with Coquelin *aîné*.

In 1899 Sarah signed a twenty-five-year lease for the Théâtre des Nations, which she re-named the Théâtre Sarah-Bernhardt.

Duval. Instead of writing her letter to Armand, Marguerite wrote: 'You're wonderful, *mon Coq*'. And she addressed the envelope 'À Coquelin'. The Brussels audience was deeply moved by Marguerite's distress.

To the end of her long and arduous life, Sarah remained untiring. She would act till midnight, change when the curtain fell, and rehearse till five in the morning. Every morning, when she rose, she would throw off her nightclothes and exercise on a stationary bicycle in her bedroom (there was also a fixed 'rowing boat' in the boulevard Péreire). She did many things, and indeed she learned many things – among them sculpture, painting and music – not so much for themselves as because of their value for the theatre. Sarah, as she said herself, was no musician; but music increased her sense of rhythm and gave her the control of

174

The Théâtre Sarah-Bernhardt programme for 1906–7 shows
a scene from *La Vierge d'Avila*.

breathing which was as necessary for elocution as it was for singing.

The theatre was the sum and centre of her interests. It was her true and perpetual home. Her life was spent upon the boards acting, and in rehearsing when she was not acting. That was all that counted. Day after day she would be in the theatre before noon, and stay there for twelve or fourteen hours, using every moment to the full. She would eat her frugal *déjeuner* and dinner in her dressing-room 'with no relief of silence, and with little interruption of the flow of business'. Sometimes in her work she was guided by impulse; but method was her mainstay, and concentration the key to it all.

In the early years of the new century, in his monograph on Sarah, Dani Busson recorded with amazement:

The trouble Sarah Bernhardt takes with the colour of a theatre poster or the shape of the sceptre of a Byzantine empress, indicates what importance she gives to every detail in her theatre.

She knows the smallest wheels in the delicate machine, and knows at once where to find the grain of sand which may prevent it from working smoothly....

She is often in the theatre in the morning; she is always there in the afternoon. You see her everywhere in the theatre. She stages the new play, indicates the gestures and the tones, reviews, rehearses, busies herself with everyone and with each individual, discusses things with the author, the electrician, the scene-shifter, the property manager, the wardrobe manager, the hairdresser and the cast, finds fault with her friends, her son, the specialists whom she sometimes brings in. You think she is about to collapse,... but you find her again in her *loge*, lying on a sofa or even on a carpet.... She has the gift which Napoleon had of going to sleep and waking up at will. A few minutes of determined sleep, and there she is, refreshed! Now, patiently, she shows the supernumeraries how to make up and do their hair and dress; she deals with the most complex affairs, or reviews the accounts of the theatre with her devoted secretary-general, M. Léon Jué, one of her oldest collaborators; then she gives auditions, has letters read to her, dictates an answer to each of them, makes enquiries about everything, talks to her friends, receives people who come for help, gives interviews....

An author who asked her to hear his play was promptly invited to follow her to London and read it there; and when, nothing daunted, he arrived, he was bidden to call at midnight and to read it to Mme Bernhardt at her hotel.

In London Sarah rehearsed in the mornings, performed in the evenings, and spent the afternoons in the suburbs giving matinées. On one

Sarah Bernhardt in later life. From a photograph by Riant.

ABOVE 'Mrs Campbell played Mélisande, Mme Bernhardt Pelléas; they are both old enough to know better.' Mrs Patrick Campbell and Sarah Bernhardt in *Pelléas et Mélisande*, by Maurice Maeterlinck, 1905.

OPPOSITE Sarah Bernhardt and Lily Langtry. From a photograph by Sarony.

occasion she performed *La Dame aux camélias* at Croydon; then she returned to London and dined at her hotel before the evening perform-ance of *Lysiane*. She ate two fried eggs and a little cold beef, and drank Apollinaris water and whisky. The mayor of Croydon, so she said, had been delightfully attentive. He had carried an armchair across the rail-way line so that she should not have to stand as she waited for the train. Such precautions seemed unnecessary. Sarah hardly seemed in need of rest. She could not, it seems, even disembark at Folkestone without giving a series of electric 'flying performances'. She never paused. 'I remember', wrote a biographer, 'the surprise of an English teacher from whom Sarah proposed taking lessons in order to play Shakespeare in English. "Mlle Bernhardt, I would gladly give you lessons, but I can spare but half an hour a day." "Well then," said she, "you must try to let me have the half hour from 2 to 2.30 a.m., for it is the only time I am not engaged." '

The part that Sarah had in mind was that of Lady Macbeth. She thought that she would like to play it in English, a language of which she could never master the rudiments. Rather improbably she engaged a Dutch lady who lived at Versailles, a Mme de Guythères. Mme de Guythères gave her one lesson. Sarah was an enthusiastic and pains-taking pupil; but when her would-be teacher arrived to give her a second lesson one of Sarah's periodical bankruptcies had happened, and she was selling her furniture and starting for America. This was not the last time that Sarah attempted to learn English. When Maurice Baring stayed with her at Belle-Île in 1901, she was studying a Shakespeare part in the original. He believed that it was Romeo.

Coquelin's departure for the Porte-Saint-Martin (of which he was co-manager) led Sarah to abandon *L'Aiglon* early in 1902, and on 22 April she created the title-part in *Francesca da Rimini*; but it was de Max, as Giovanni Malatesta, who earned the applause.

Nor did she gain spectacular success when, in October, just before her fifty-eighth birthday, she first appeared before the Berlin public. For years the Germans had implored her to play in Germany; and for years she had rigorously avoided Germany on her tours. When a Ger-man manager asked her her terms for performing *L'Aiglon* in Berlin, she had simply cabled back 'Alsace-Lorraine'.

And so she did not play now to tumultuous houses. But at least she played to full ones; and when Wilhelm II invited her to Potsdam and

A moment of inexplicable drama: Sarah Bernhardt outside the stage door of the Vaudeville Theatre, London, in 1904.

gave a luncheon in her honour, she added another monarch to her score of regal admirers.

The years 1902 and 1903 were not entirely successful for Sarah, and only in December 1903 did she achieve an uncontested success (her last with Sardou) in *La Sorcière*.

On 8 April 1905 she played Assuérus in a revival of *Esther*; and at the end of the month she left for London, where she played in Maurice Maeterlinck's *Pelléas et Mélisande* for the first time. Mrs Patrick Campbell, who had already played Mélisande in English in England and the United States, now played it in French to Sarah's Pelléas. Alas, when they took the play on tour, a Dublin critic wrote succinctly: 'Mrs Campbell played Mélisande, Mme Bernhardt Pelléas. They are both old enough to know better'.

5
The Stricken
Queen

During her American tour of 1905–6, Sarah Bernhardt was sometimes obliged to give her performance in a tent. Here she is seen outside her tent at Dallas, Texas.

ON 5 JUNE 1905 Sarah embarked at Southampton for yet another American tour. On 9 October, at Rio de Janeiro, she met with one of the great disasters of her life. She was playing in *La Tosca*. At the end of the last scene Floria committed suicide by leaping off the parapet of the Castel Sant' Angelo. Usually, of course, the stage behind the parapet was covered with mattresses; that night, for some unknown reason, the mattresses had been forgotten, and Sarah fell heavily on her right knee. She fainted with pain; her leg swelled violently, and she was carried to her hotel on a stretcher. Next day, when she embarked for New York, a doctor was called to her state-room, but his hands were so dirty that she refused to let him touch her. In vain her friends protested, insisted that they would make him take a bath. Sarah would see no doctor until she reached New York three weeks later.

Her New York season had to be postponed for a fortnight. In about mid-November, she was able to walk and to begin her tour in Chicago. But the three weeks' delay had proved disastrous; and, inexorably, her injury grew worse. By 1908 she could only walk with difficulty; by 1911 she could not walk unsupported; by 1913 the furniture had to be arranged on stage so that she never took more than two consecutive steps. In her dressing-room she rubbed ether on her knee to deaden the pain; often she was given injections. And as she walked to her entrance she was helped by a handrail of rope round the back of the stage. When she made her exit she would fall exhausted into a chair and rest for several minutes before she was taken back to her dressing-room. Some say that her knee became tubercular; it is certain that after her accident in 1905 it gave her increasing pain.

Meanwhile, on this American tour of 1905–6, she visited some sixty-two cities, and the crowds flocked to see her, thinking that it might be for the last time. Since Sarah refused to bow to the demands of the American Theatre Trust, she was obliged to perform in tents, tabernacles and skating rinks. One evening, so the story goes, at Omaha, Nebraska, a cowboy arrived at the gallop, tethered his horse to a tree and demanded a seat. He had ridden 300 miles to see her. As he raised the flap of the tent, he asked the cashier: 'By the way, what does this Bernhardt do – dance or sing?'

Late in June 1906 Sarah Bernhardt returned to France, went to London for three weeks; and then, tired and ill, spent a couple of months at

Belle-Île dictating her torrential, charming and frequently inaccurate *Mémoires*. Punctuation, said Sarah, was largely concerned with the written word. On stage one must follow the thought and phrase accordingly. Years of this practice did not help the writing of her memoirs. But then, as Sarah herself observed: '*Tant pis, on n'est pas grammairienne!*' There were, of course, some readers who remained convinced that Sarah had not written the book herself. But they were promptly silenced by Max Beerbohm. 'Let writers console themselves with the reflection that to Sarah all things are possible.... [No hack] could have imparted to the book the peculiar fire and salt that it has – the rushing spontaneity that stamps it, for every discriminating reader, as Sarah's own.'

How astonishing, how admirable were these, her later years! The injured, defiant child of years ago, who had taken as her motto the challenge *Quand même*, had become the injured, ageing, but indomitable woman. And when, in May 1909, the actress Adeline Dudlay gave her farewell performance, Sarah made her only reappearance in the rue de Richelieu. She was sixty-four and she took the part of the young Romantic poet in *La Nuit de mai* by Alfred de Musset. That November, defiant as ever, she took the name part in *Le Procès de Jeanne d'Arc*. Twenty years earlier, in her forties, in a play by Jules Barbier, she had appeared as the Maid of Orleans. Now, at sixty-five, she played Joan of Arc again; and when, in the trial scene, she was asked her age, she turned slowly, very slowly, to face the audience. Gently but firmly she answered: 'Nineteen'. Every evening, at this point, she was given an ovation.

May Agate, who saw the play, found the final moments, the death at the stake, too realistic to be borne. She knew enough about the theatre to be well aware that the effects were being worked by stage hands, that Sarah herself was sitting in a chair behind a 'flat', waiting for the cue to cry '*Jésus!*' But Sarah had already created such a compelling portrait of Jeanne that the audience was carried away, and for a moment they thought that Jeanne was there, suffering torture in the red glow of the final curtain.

Fiercely, delightedly, Sarah moved with the times. Once she had gone up in a balloon to defy authority; now she risked the pleasure of being rude to the telephone operator (and was cut off for days in consequence). In 1908 she had filmed *La Tosca* in the market-hall of Belleville (it was a poor film, even judged by the standards of the day). *La*

Sarah Bernhardt as Jeanne d'Arc. She played the part in Jules Barbier's play of that name (1890) and again in *Le Procès de Jeanne d'Arc* by Émile Moreau (1909). In this second play she took the rôle of the girl of nineteen when she herself had reached the respectable age of sixty-five.

Dame aux camélias was later filmed at Neuilly; but this, to Sarah's mind, was also a failure, and she hated to hear it mentioned. But other films followed: *La Reine Élisabeth* (1911); *Adrienne Lecouvreur* (1912); and in 1913 *Madame Sarah Bernhardt at Home*. Sarah was one of the few to recognize in the new-born cinema the embryo of the giant it would become.

Such modernity was characteristic of Sarah. She did not disdain to appear, for the first time in her life, as a London music-hall attraction; and that summer of 1910 in London, at the Coliseum, a Turkey red carpet eighty feet long was laid from Sarah's dressing-room to the stage, so that her feet should not touch the boards which, perhaps, performing

187

Queen Sarah: a scene from a sumptuous *fin de siècle* production.

elephants had just trodden. But would Rachel, would Irving have condescended so far?

In 1912 an aviator, demonstrating his skill with his primitive aircraft, flew over Sarah's fort at Belle-Île. He dropped a bunch of flowers at the foot of the mast where her personal flag was flying – embroidered with her motto 'Quand même'. That year, on 23 October, Sarah would be sixty-eight, and her English admirers prepared to celebrate her birthday. A reporter from *The Daily Telegraph* called at Belle-Île to tell her; and moved, surprised, she recalled her debt to the English public.

For a third of a century now, almost every year, she had crossed the Channel, finding her best friends among the compatriots of Shakespeare. It was London, she said, that had taught her to have confidence in herself, to leave the Comédie-Française and to trust her own wings. England had launched her. And she liked to recall how Queen Victoria had received her and approved of her performance of Marguerite Gautier, given it the brevet of respectability.

Sarah often observed that 'in Paris they go to the theatre, in London they rush there'. To Sir George Arthur, a friend and admirer who later published his impressions of her, she said that the British public was the most faithful in the world. She believed that if she appeared on a London stage and her voice failed, she would still be applauded in memory of what she had done. But as the years passed and she showed signs of age, Paris had become critical almost to the point of cruelty. She felt it had little indulgence for her. Perhaps the French were slow to forgive her for leaving the Comédie-Française and making a triumph of her independence. Only now, when her health was clearly beginning to fail, did her compatriots appreciate what she had done for France.

It had been in London that Sarah had married Damala; and every succeeding summer she had installed herself at the Metropole, the Carlton or the Savoy, where, at lunchtime, she received all her friends: Lord Glenesk, who was always among the first to welcome her; Oscar Wilde, whose wit so delighted her; and Ellen Terry. Sarah had watched Sargent in his studio; she had bowled down Knightsbridge in her carriage to visit Burne-Jones. She longed, in vain, for Burne-Jones to paint her portrait; but he could not overcome his dislike of painting portraits, even to paint her covered with jewels as Théodora.

'Miss Sarah and I have always been able to understand one another,' wrote Ellen Terry. Irving, it is true, did not understand her so well. He grew much attached to her, and he admired her as a colleague for her managerial work in the theatre; but of her powers as an actress (considered Ellen Terry) 'I don't believe he ever had a glimmering notion'. But whatever Irving's self-absorption (and he never enjoyed the acting of others), Sarah had made an ineffaceable impression upon the English public. 'We say Sarah', wrote A. B. Walkley, after her death, 'as our forefathers said Rachel. It is a tribute to greatness, as you call a pope Innocent or a king George. Sarah was without peer as a great institution.'

Nor had she only conquered London. When, after her performance of Pelléas in Maeterlinck's play, she walked through the garden of the Midland Hotel in Manchester, supported by two Florentine lackeys, 'hard-headed cotton manufacturers who had never heard of her stood up and removed their hats, and common stockbrokers, abashed and open-mouthed, left their stories in the air'. In Manchester she performed yet again in *La Dame aux camélias*. Never did her playing seem more authentic. When Sarah, as Marguerite Gautier, left Armand, the audience longed to call out to him: 'Don't let her go! She won't come back!' You were carried away, so May Agate remembered. There was

OVERLEAF Sarah Bernhardt returns from a tour of America (1910); her granddaughter Lysiane Bernhardt is carrying a coat, on the left.

no resisting such acting. It had the power and sincerity of life. May
Agate herself had watched the last act a score of times; and on more
than one occasion she and her mother had waited in Sarah's dressing-
room until she had her call. She knew that Sarah switched on the part
like an electric fire. Yet so perfect was the technique that every time she
was convinced anew of the reality. And so, too, was their old family
doctor. One day they took him to see the play at the Manchester Hippodrome. He kept criticizing the criminal folly of letting a tubercular
patient have visitors. For him the very air was germ-laden.

It was, perhaps, from Manchester that there came the nicest story
of Sarah in England: a story that showed her Frenchness and her anglo-
philia to perfection. One afternoon when she was performing in Manchester she took a drive with a friend into the country. As they were
passing a field they heard shouts and stopped the landau. Two local
football teams were playing a match. Sarah climbed up on to the seat
and, clad from head to foot in white furs, watched the contest with
eager interest. When it was over she climbed down and sank back into
her cushions with a murmured: '*J'adore ce cricket: c'est tellement anglais.*'

It was to this favourite England that Sarah came, now, late in August
1912, insisting again, as she had always insisted, on the need for an
English National Theatre. Matthew Arnold had heard her plead for
it in 1879; and he had long recalled 'a fugitive vision of delicate features
under a shower of hair and a cloud of lace'; he had long heard 'the
voice of Mlle Sarah Bernhardt saying in its most caressing terms to the
Londoners: "The theatre is irresistible; *organize the theatre!*"' That had
been over thirty years ago; and now 'what you want', she told a journalist, 'is a real National Theatre in London, with substantial aid from
public funds. Every nation ought to have such a theatre. Private enterprise cannot give it to you.... You have the good fortune to have a
national dramatist. Why not a National Theatre?'

Madame Sarah herself, that incarnation of private enterprise, now
performed again at the Coliseum. On 7 October, at the King's Hall,
Holborn Restaurant, a midnight reception and theatre show were held
in her honour; and when she left for the Carlton Hotel in the small
hours of the morning, 'she sat back in a motor brougham half-filled
with magnificent bouquets'. On 10 October, on the stage of the Coliseum, Ellen Terry gave her two bouquets and said: 'Queen Sarah, you
have no more devoted subject than Ellen Terry'. Sarah seemed a brilli-

ant flame of elemental passion and emotion. Ellen, with her failing sight, seemed like a soft light that had once illumined the theatre. It was no doubt this afternoon that May Agate saw them together on the stage. Sarah could hardly stand without pain, but she was still full of her golden dignity. Ellen was 'fumbling her way pathetically about but still, at heart, something of a hoyden'. Sarah, wrote May Agate, was 'exotic, flamboyant, compelling, suggesting the hothouse; Ellen speaking to us of the open air, the English lanes and fields, and now of home and the fireside. And these two women in some curious way cancelled each other out like a sky holding sun and moon together.'

On 23 October, her sixty-eighth birthday, in a cloak of white satin and sable, Sarah attended a reception at the Savoy. A hundred thousand admirers had filled three volumes with their signatures, and signatures were still pouring in. And Sarah's English lessons had, it seemed, borne sudden fruit. In the only English speech she ever made, she rejoiced that art had laid the foundations of *l'entente cordiale*.

Only a hand at the window: Sarah Bernhardt
sets out by train from the Gare du Nord on yet another triumphal tour.

'The Empire's tribute to Sarah Bernhardt: a birthday celebration
at the Savoy.' An English artist's impression of the reception held
in London on 23 October 1912, her sixty-eighth birthday.

Georges Clemenceau, politician and patriot
(1841–1929). An admirer of Sarah Bernhardt's, he
persuaded her to seek safety outside Paris when the
First World War was declared.

   Sarah's devotion to the theatre did not prevent her from taking a constant interest in all that was happening on the larger stage of politics.
She delighted in talking to politicians and statesmen, and had her lot
been differently cast she would no doubt have revelled in a *salon*. She
read the papers closely, skimming gossip, we are told, but studying significant events. No one could question her patriotism. In her long and
brilliant life she met many kings and princes; but her delight in,
and reverence for them, in no way conflicted with her republicanism. She
was a fervent republican, largely because she was convinced that a republic was the only form of government for France, and what was best
for France must be good elsewhere. Sir George Arthur wrote that 'she
carried her republicanism to the edge, though not across the border,
of socialism. Her idea of socialism was probably somewhat vague, and
would suggest an infinite opportunity for everyone to be happy. If only
she could rule the world, she would say, the world should be a paradise.

Pain and poverty should be banished – pleasure and sunshine should be permanent – beauty should be everywhere.'

And so it was that her charity knew no frontiers. She did good without thinking of nationalities or religions, political or social differences. In 1904, with Caruso, she had organized a performance of *Rigoletto* in aid of the Russian wounded in the Russo-Japanese War. More recently, in America, she had given two performances in aid of the victims of an earthquake. Sarah was often praised for her kindness of heart; and she did good wherever there was affliction.

On 15 January 1914 the President of the French Republic paid an official visit to the Théâtre Sarah-Bernhardt. He watched Sarah's performance in *Jeanne Doré*, and he invested her with the insignia awarded to every dutiful French functionary : the cross of Chevalier de la Légion-d'honneur. 'Dear great friend,' cabled Rostand, 'I kiss you with all my heart' ; and in a second telegram he added: 'Every poet and artist has waited impatiently for the time when your huge mass of laurels should at last be bound by this little bit of red ribbon.' The Minister of Public Instruction later recalled her qualifications for the honour. 'Sarah Bernhardt served as a hospital nurse in the war of 1870, and she has made the French tongue known throughout the world.'

Soon afterwards, Maurice Baring saw Sarah in *La Dame aux camélias*.

She was suffering from her leg. . . . The stage had to be marked out in chalk for her, showing the spots where she could stand up, for she was too unwell to stand up for more than certain given moments. I went to see her with a Russian actress who had seen her play in Russia and had not been able to endure her acting, thinking it affected and listless, and wondering what her reputation was founded on. We arrived late, after the second act, and I went behind the scenes and talked to Sarah, and told her of this Russian actress who was tone-deaf to her art. Sarah played the last three acts with such agonizing poignancy and reserve, that not only was my Russian friend in tears, but the actors on the stage cried so much that their tears discoloured their faces and made runnels in their grease-paint. I said I never would see her act again after that, and I did not.

There was little chance to see her perform. In May she began to tour France with *Jeanne Doré*, but her performances were interrupted at Lille, near the Belgian frontier, and on 28 July she returned to Paris. Within a week the First World War had begun.

Sarah spent August in Paris. She was suffering greatly from her knee

OVERLEAF Sarah Bernhardt's Paris: a photograph taken on the boulevards at the turn of the century.

and hardly left the boulevard Péreire. Late that month her family advised her to leave Paris, but she refused to listen to them. It took Georges Clemenceau himself to force her to the decision. Clemenceau (who, at the time, was out of politics) had been warned by the counterespionage authorities that Sarah was on the list of hostages who were to be deported if the Germans took the capital. At that time many Frenchmen believed that the Germans would come back to Paris; and Clemenceau, reminding her of her family, her theatre and its employees, her own unique importance to her country, at last persuaded her to seek safety. On 31 August she set off in her car for the south.

She had rented a villa at Andernos, about twenty-five miles from Bordeaux, and there she settled indefinitely; as the war news improved she would have liked to go back to Paris in October, but her knee had grown far worse and it was giving her acute pain. Her leg was put in plaster. After three months of immobility, it was found that the disease was no longer local but was actually threatening her life. Professor Pozzi came from Paris to consult with two local doctors; and after lengthy consultations they suggested amputation. 'Since there is nothing else to be done,' said Sarah, 'why ask my opinion?'

She herself decided on the amputation.

My father [remembered Maurice Rostand] went to Bordeaux for this sensational operation. Pozzi and Doyen refused to perform it, and only Major Denucé of the hospital at Bordeaux was prepared to risk it.

I have often spoken of Sarah's courage. It is not excessive to call it her heroism. We saw it there, above all. Was the amputation inevitable? Was there not in this determined resolution a kind of unspoken need to conform to the rhythm of the age and to become an invalid like – alas – so many young men of the time?

At the age of seventy, with remarkable courage, she prepared herself for the operation that was to deprive her for ever of Rostand's epithet '*Reine de l'attitude, princesse des gestes*'. On the eve of the operation she sent a characteristic telegram to a friend in Paris: 'To-morrow they are going to take off my leg. Think of me, and book me some lectures for April.'

She was forced to spend about a fortnight in bed at Bordeaux before she went back to Andernos for her convalescence. She was already thinking of playing *La Princesse lointaine*, with Ida Rubinstein as Geof-

Sarah Bernhardt in her study: a photograph
taken towards the end of the century.

Sarah Bernhardt performing in *Mères françaises*, outside Rheims
Cathedral, in 1916. This photograph shows her after her operation,
when she was unable to stand unaided.

frey Rudel; and Queen Alexandra, who sent a message of sympathy,
received a brisk if grateful acknowledgment: 'Madame, I make use of
the first minute that the doctor permits me to think, to express my deep
gratitude to Your Gracious Majesty.' No woman, Sarah once said, need
be as old as her years, but only so old as she thinks herself. 'The same
applies to death. I often think about death, but only to assure myself
that I shall not die until I am ready.'

   She was not ready yet. She needed once more to lose herself in art.
'I accept being maimed,' she wrote, 'but I refuse to remain powerless.
Work is my life.' In October she returned to Paris and arranged a series

'Houdini, you do such wonderful things. Could you bring back my
leg for me?' Sarah Bernhardt with Harry Houdini, the magician of
magicians, during her American tour of 1916–18.

of matinées for charity; her own part was to be that of Strasbourg Cathedral in a scenic poem by Eugène Morand: *Les Cathédrales*.

She was never able to walk again after she lost her leg; she was never
able even to stand on an artificial limb. Wherever she went she was
carried in a folding chair; she travelled in a specially built car. She
was so philosophical herself that she probably did not know how dis-
tressing it was for others to see her disabled. May Agate and her mother
went to Sarah's dressing-room after the first performance of *Les Cathédrales*. They found Olga Nethersole, the actress, kneeling before her and
sobbing her heart out. Sarah was holding her hands and soothing her.

Sarah Bernhardt at seventy-three.
From a photograph taken in America in 1917.

'But Olga, my dear, you mustn't take on so. I am all right now, I feel
wonderful. There, there. . . .' Sarah could never bear the sight of tears.

And so she lost herself in work, and she appeared as a nurse in a
topical film, *Mères françaises*. In the spring of 1916 she was carried round
the front and performed for the Théâtre des Armées. On 30 September
she embarked once again, this time with a very small company, for
America. She took a new repertory to suit her condition, including the
third act of *Le Procès de Jeanne d'Arc*, the fifth act of *La Dame aux camélias*,
the sixth act of *L'Aiglon*. Early in 1918 she returned to France. As she
crossed the Atlantic, the submarines were busy. Sarah was informed

Sarah Bernhardt, aged seventy-four, arrives to recite
to the *poilus* at the Front in 1918.

of the danger, but she stayed in her cabin, and a visitor found her
absorbed in a game of dominoes.

She. was brave; but she returned to France weary and discouraged,
knowing how disappointed the public must have been by her mediocre
repertory, and saddened by the thought of the plays that were now
forbidden her. One day in America she had met the magician of magicians, Harry Houdini. 'Houdini, you do such wonderful things,' she
had said to him. 'Could you bring back my leg for me?' And, seeing
that he was startled, she added: 'Yes, but you do the impossible. I never
was more serious in my life.'

205

6
Final
Offering

Sarah Bernhardt photographed at home in 1906.

IN 1920 SARAH GAVE a series of special performances of Racine's *Athalie*. She was carried on to the stage in a golden palanquin. Paul Géraldy, the poet and playwright, stood in the wings and saw her as she passed. She looked decrepit, a very old woman with chattering teeth and withered face. But no sooner had she said the opening lines than he felt the spell which she had cast over the whole theatre. Her voice became the gate of a hundred sorrows, and her eyes had in them the retrospect and the sadness of resurrected spring. He and all the audience were ready to kneel at her feet and to weep.

It was this year that May Agate saw Sarah again in Paris. She was carried into the drawing-room in the boulevard Péreire, and May Agate found her enormously changed. Her hair was now allowed to be its own natural white. She wore it loosely tied with a black bow. Her features had always been fine, but they were now more rugged than before; and, for the first time, she looked old.

Maurice Rostand, too, remembered Sarah in these latter days.

Old, with only one leg – she was now seventy-six – she wore these numberless years with a white satin dress and the eyes of the *Jeune homme à la houlette* by Van Dyck, which, indeed, Marcel Proust considered she resembled. She invited us, imperiously, to come to *déjeuner*, and we did not dream of disobeying this old empress of the theatre, who commanded with a smile. She was still living opposite the suburban railway, the *chemin de fer de ceinture*, in the small *hôtel* in the boulevard Péreire.... It was cluttered with every kind of furniture, and you found some of the worst bric-à-brac alongside some fine pieces. The *déjeuners* at Sarah's were ordered like meals on stage. She made her appearance suddenly, with her back to the light, sitting on a kind of Gothic chair which she occupied before we entered so that we should not see her carried on a stretcher – though, with her, the stretcher would have seemed the litter of Athalie. The guests were nearly always the same.... There was her son Maurice, ... who looked so unlike the director of a theatre, and was indeed so unlike a director. He had lost his first wife, the beautiful Polish woman, and he had married again – this time a charming Parisian. There was Sarah's granddaughter, Lysiane, like some stylized portrait of Sarah's youth which had come to life again. There was a maid of honour, ready for everything; she had replaced poor [Mlle] Seylor, who had been dismissed in a moment of anger; the maid of honour was called Mme de Gournay....

There was also Arthur Meyer, the journalist, who had worshipped Sarah since the days of *Le Passant*. Now he was crimped and sterile,

with a waxen face, like some tame poodle who wanted to look like a familiar

209

Sarah Bernhardt: a photograph taken on her private train in America, 1912.

in distinguished circles. There was Reynaldo Hahn, who sang so well, even other people's music. Diane-Valentine Feydeau, the sister of Georges, an amazon with a man's heart whose friendship had its worth. As for Louise Abbéma, who wore an enormous rosette, she always seemed like an old Japanese general who had not committed harakiri. . . .

The *déjeuners* were unlike any others. We talked of everything. Sarah's memories seemed to go back to the Flood. She was charming and fierce, she was capable of the worst compliments and the most subtle cruelties.

She held out her hand to Arthur Meyer – a little, square, energetic hand on which all the rings of Lalique had been assembled. And she whispered to him, as if it were an exquisite invitation: 'Well, dear Tutur, when shall we decide to die?' The question made her laugh till the tears came to her eyes. It made old Tutur turn pale to the depths of his soul, supposing that he had one.

On Saturday 4 April 1921 she arrived in London. On the way to Boulogne her car had broken down, and she had been forced to spend the night at Montreuil-sur-Mer and to leave there at five in the morning. The crossing had been rough, and she reached the Savoy in a state of exhaustion.

Two hours later, she was rehearsing; for on Monday she was to perform at the Princes Theatre in *Daniel*.

That Monday, immediately before the second act, she was carried on to the stage; and there she remained until the final curtain; and *Daniel* 'was wonderful, though more wonderful still was the intense emotion of the whole house while waiting for the curtain to go up'. Children who heard little and could understand less were brought to the theatre so that they might say one day that they had seen Sarah Bernhardt. For older generations, it was a strange evening of reminiscence 'overlaying and almost obliterating experience'. It was today that Sarah was promoted Officier de la Légion-d'honneur; and it was today that, led by Ellen Terry, the English acting profession gave her a golden book of signatures in homage and gratitude.

'You ask me my theory of life,' said Sarah once. 'It is represented by the word *will*. . . . Life is short, even for those who live a long time, and we must live for the few who know and appreciate us, who judge and absolve us, and for whom we have the same affection and indulgence. We ought to hate very rarely, as it is too fatiguing, remain indifferent a great deal, forgive often, and never forget.'

Synopsis
and ::
Press
Book

KILNER'S
EXCLUSIVE
FILMS, Ltd.
26, LITCHFIELD STREET,
CHARING CROSS ROAD,
W.C. 2.

Telephone : Regent 875 & 876.
Telegrams : "Superfilms, London."
Cables : Western Union & Marconi Codes.

Sarah Bernhardt – as this poster modestly reminds us – was among
the first to recognize the potential of the cinema.

I remember seeing Sarah on her last visit to London [wrote an acquaintance],
driving in a victoria at Hyde Park Corner. As she leaned back in the carriage,
extravagantly pale, and with the lamp-black an inch thick under the eyes and
on her eyelids, she looked lovelier than the fairest beauty of the season. She
took you into a world where fresh senses were accorded. Did one love this
woman? Yes, but as that passion may be conceived on some other planet.
What one felt began with admiration and ended there. One desired her just
as much and just as little as one desires Cleopatra or Helen of Troy.

Still, in the final stages of life and infirmity, she gave a strange illusion
of youth and beauty. Soon afterwards she invited C. B. Cochran to

tea with her in Paris; and he had 'seldom passed a more wonderful hour. After five minutes I felt that this wonderful woman was not old and crippled, but beautiful and young.... She asked where was the successor of our Irving and our adorable Ellen Terry? She spoke with affection and admiration of the Guitrys. Lucien, she said, was the sole survivor of the great actors of the past. She was enormously interested in the progress of Yvonne Printemps...'

She was interested in everything. She performed at a gala in aid of Mme Curie, *la femme radium;* she considered a tour of Holland, began negotiations for a tour of the Americas. At Belle-Île she entertained a company of film-actors working on Dumas' *Twenty Years After.* And then, once more, she turned to art. In October she appeared as Glory in Maurice Rostand's *La Gloire.* In October 1922, after a tour in Italy, she took up *La Gloire* again. She could only take parts, now, in which she was motionless: *La Gloire,* in which she appeared in a frame; *Athalie,* in which she rested on a litter. She was nearing eighty and sometimes death must have seemed long in coming.

On 25 October 1922, as she prepared in her dressing-room for *La Gloire,* she was overcome by the shuddering that announced an attack of uremia. The doctor forbade her to perform that evening; but 'when the hour comes, she for whom the Swedes sowed the waves of the Baltic with roses, beneath whose feet the Peruvians spread their cloaks, must, like her comrades, obey the call of the prompter. There lies her salvation.' And there lay Sarah's duty. Devoted to Maurice Rostand, she continued like a soldier of the theatre. And then the curtain fell between her and the world, enveloping her like a great purple shroud.

In December, rehearsing a play by Sacha Guitry, *Un Sujet de roman,* she collapsed. Her first words when she regained consciousness were: 'When shall I appear again?' She did not succumb at once. A week later she attended the dress rehearsal of *Le Phénix* by Maurice Rostand, and all Paris filed through her dressing-room in homage. But she had presumed too much on her strength; and from that moment she began to fail.

On 15 March 1923 Lysiane Bernhardt arrived at the boulevard Péreire to watch the filming of *La Voyante.* In the studio, facing networks of scaffolding, mercury lights and spotlights, was a décor of a fortune-teller's booth with a view of Montmartre from the window; and Sarah sat weary, expressionless, behind a table. Patiently she picked up her fortune-telling cards and went through her movements. Then she fell.

Sarah Bernhardt at home, 1917.

Sarah Bernhardt's funeral, Maundy Thursday,
1923. The cortège passes the Théâtre Sarah-
Bernhardt on its way to Père-Lachaise.

Sarah Bernhardt's tomb at Père-Lachaise.

Long ago she had told the Duchess of Teck: '*Altesse Royale, je mourrai en scène: c'est mon champ de bataille.*'

On 20 March the doctors declared that the poison had entered her system and that there was no hope. At first she was in despair. She had wanted to perform in Guitry's new play; she had wanted to finish her film. Then, gradually, she grew resigned, and resignation turned to torpor, and those around her knew that Sarah was going to die.

She knew it too. She knew that the journalists were waiting night and day on the bench in the boulevard Péreire facing her windows. It amused her to keep them waiting. On 23 March Mrs Patrick Campbell came to dinner and found her wearing a long-sleeved dress of pink Venetian velvet sent by Sacha Guitry. Knowing that she had not long

216

to live, Sarah sat there, white-faced, eating nothing and infinitely gracious. When dinner was over, she was carried upstairs on her chair; turning the bend of the staircase, she kissed one finger and held it out.

'How slow death is in coming,' she said to Maurice on the morning of 26 March; and again, '*Je veux des fleurs, beaucoup de fleurs*. It is springtime, let me have a wealth of flowers.' She had moments of serenity, moments of lucidity; moments, too, of delirium, when she recalled the great deaths she had played: the death of Marguerite Gautier, the death of l'Aiglon. And wildly, now, in identification, she recited the words.

At half past three that afternoon she received extreme unction; and at five past eight, in a deep coma, she died.

Sarah, who had received so many flowers in her life, was given them in death. Her pillow was covered with roses and white and purple lilac, her death-bed was surrounded by lilac and roses, forget-me-nots and Parma violets. The multitudes who came to see her walked through a house that seemed a very garden, into a room impassable for flowers.

Sarah was dressed, as l'Aiglon had been dressed, in white. She wore a white satin robe; on her breast was the insignia of the Légion-d'honneur, and round her neck was a gold locket on a black ribbon, holding a portrait of Maurice, a lock of his hair. In her hands was a crucifix of gold and ebony, and 'her face, full of peace, was like carved ivory'.

And then she was laid in the rosewood coffin, lined with old rose satin, that had waited so long.

Sarah Bernhardt was buried on Maundy Thursday, 1923, at Père-Lachaise. She was buried with proper splendour, and with a wealth of flowers. At the time of her funeral in Paris, the authorities of Belle-Île went to Les Poulains and laid a sheaf of flowers on the drawbridge of her fort. The sailors at Sauzon had already strewn it with camellias. A wreath was cast into the sea by the great rock where Sarah had asked to be buried.

After her death the fort and the château were sold. In October 1944, during the Occupation, the German military authorities blew up the château which Sarah had once been tempted to destroy.

Sarah Bernhardt, aged seventy-five, with her bust of Edmond Rostand.
From a photograph taken in her studio in the boulevard Péreire, 1919.

7
Curtain Call

SARAH BERNHARDT lived in and for and by the theatre. She was the most professional of actresses. Throughout her career she concerned herself with the grand scope and the minute detail of her art.

May Agate set down some of Sarah's precepts for the benefit of posterity. Never shock the spectator, said Sarah, by the abruptness of your speech or gesture. Register the thought before the action. Prepare the audience. Remember the significance of pauses. Silence on stage is more eloquent than anything else in the theatre. Once, said Sarah, when her audience was crying too much over Marguerite Gautier, she had paused in mid performance, and they were silent. An actor could always control his audience with a measured pause. If, however, he should pause for any other purpose, he must fill his pause with silent acting. His mind must work, and show that it was working all the time. When you studied a part, you must never stop thinking about it. You must immerse yourself in it as you went about your daily life. If it became second nature to you, your characteristic touches would come by instinct.

Sarah insisted, repeatedly, on correctness of detail. Only the need to economize drove her, on one occasion, to use dark-haired children as the Austrian cousins of l'Aiglon; but dark-haired extras were cheaper than fair ones in the theatre. And if Émile Moreau's drama, *La Reine Élisabeth*, was the worst failure that she ever knew, it was not for want of local colour. As the play opened, Sarah was seen eating '*du plom cake*' with a two-pronged silver fork. She could only bring herself (May Agate remembered) to swallow about two currants and a raisin, 'but she put up a very good fight, and thought she was being tremendously British'. Sarah was sometimes unconvincing, but she was undoubtedly determined. Once, at a dress rehearsal, she herself 'broke in' a pair of new boots which a child extra was wearing. She mixed Fuller's earth and grease-paint to represent mud and worked it into the offending leather.

The actress who had studied anatomy in the dissecting-room insisted on accurate clinical detail. In *Julie* she died from a heart condition. Her choking was not the tubercular choking of Marguerite Gautier, and a doctor would have noticed the difference. She herself thought that her death in *Léna* was remarkable; it was in this death-scene that she fell flat on her face, overcome by morphine. 'I die quite well, too,' she observed to Reynaldo Hahn, 'in *Adrienne Lecouvreur*.' It was here that she died, with all too much veracity, from poison.

221

She understood the importance of historical authenticity, the importance of accurate physical detail. She understood, quite marvellously, how to suggest the nuances of emotion. Never did her playing seem more authentic than it did in *La Dame aux camélias*. Hahn remembered how she sent the producer a bunch of lilac so that she could arrange it on the stage when she and Armand Duval discussed their future. Into that arrangement of flowers she put a world of feeling. And Hahn, too, remembered the moment when Marguerite first thought of leaving Armand for ever. 'She grew pale, her lips trembled; under this mask-like pallor we could feel the tumult of her mind; the heart was beating so fast that it seemed to have stopped.... Those who have not once in their lives deliberately renounced their happiness ... do not understand what eternal quality there was in Sarah's playing.' When unexpectedly she saw the man she had renounced, Sarah murmured '*Ah! que j'ai eu tort!*' 'You cannot', said Hahn, 'understand the beauty of that tiny piece of acting unless you have once turned a corner and seen someone from whom a world divided you, someone you still loved.... It was the definitive expression of an emotion.'

Sarah herself had experienced a thousand emotions. She could identify with every part. Such was her range that, as Lorenzaccio, she became terrifyingly sinister and macabre. She seemed to be transformed on stage, to acquire superhuman strength: at one point she seized a heavy oak chair and pounded the floor with it. Such was her acting that, when she collapsed, the audience were convinced that she had actually lost consciousness. Sarah achieved her effect not so much by the actual collapse as by her subsequent playing in a minor key. She made her recovery a slow one, she played Lorenzaccio as a sick person, to emphasize the degree of the collapse. She was much amused to learn that the Agates had been deceived. 'That's how you should act, my dears!' she said.

Sarah could be fierce or ailing or miserable at will. 'I can't stop crying!' she explained when she was rehearsing Feuillet's *Julie*. 'I absolutely must make myself unhappy at rehearsals, otherwise I should be good for nothing.' Reynaldo Hahn, waiting off-stage before the last act of *Frou-Frou*, saw Sarah take up position behind the door to wait for her cue. 'I've come to upset myself', she said, 'before I make my entrance.' She kept her ear close to the door and listened to the conversation on the stage. Her eyes soon filled with tears; and, turning to Hahn, she said, almost embarrassed: 'It's really happened, I've upset myself.' She went on stage sobbing and near to death. Between two acts of a play, in the space of ten or fifteen minutes, Sarah could live six months, a week, or a night. She had an extraordinary power of identification with mood, of taking on the spirit of a play. She could sharpen her sensibility as she pleased.

She understood, too, how to imply an impending drama, to indicate the undertones of crisis. When Maurice Baring, in the 1890s, saw her play the quarrel scene in *Frou-Frou*,

> it was like watching someone skating on thin ice and knowing that they are getting nearer and nearer to peril ... It was the overtones of her play here that were so wonderful. The slight indication she gave of what was going on beneath the surface and of all that had been going on beneath the surface for months; a slow and gradually rippling tide of irritation indicated now by a tremble in the finger, a certain restlessness, a catch in the voice, or a twitch of the shoulder, and an ominous glinting of the eyes....
>
> No actor or actress ever made greater play with the eyes: now wistful and wondering ... ; now like glinting gems ... ; now blazing with fury or flooded with passion; now sad with all the sorrows of the world ...

Some said that Phèdre was the ultimate accomplishment of Sarah Bernhardt, as it had been that of Rachel. Maurice Baring maintained that 'Doña Sol was perhaps the part in which she attained the highest poetical perfection.... In the Seventies and Eighties, in Victor Hugo's *Hernani* and *Ruy Blas*, she had poetry, passion, and grace and youth, and first love to express. She expressed it easily with unerring poetical tact; there was no strain, not a harsh note, it was a symphony of golden flutes and muted strings; a summer dawn lit by lambent lightnings, soft stars, and a clear-cut crescent moon.'

And here, perhaps, we come to her unique and supreme achievement. Sarah was technically accomplished, brilliantly versatile. She was an uncompromising, superb professional; she understood every aspect of her manifold art. But, above all, she brought poetry to the theatre.

She was Théodora walking on like one of Burne-Jones' dreams, amidst the splendours of Byzantium. She was La Princesse lointaine, crowned with silver lilies, sumptuous and sad like one of Swinburne's early poems. She was Izeyl, the incarnation of an exotic sonnet by Baudelaire. She was La Samaritaine, evoking all the spices, the fire and vehemence of the Song of Solomon. She was Gismonda, with orchids and hortensia in her hair, in the jewelled glow of the Middle Ages.

Eliminate these things [wrote Baring], and you eliminate one of the sources of inspiration of modern art. You take away something from d'Annunzio's poetry, from Maeterlinck's prose, from Moreau's pictures, you destroy one of the mainsprings of Rostand's work; you annihilate some of the colours of modern painting, and you stifle some of the notes of modern music (Fauré and Hahn), for in all these things you can trace in various degrees the subtle and unconscious influence of Sarah Bernhardt.

Maurice Baring was not alone in making these claims; Dani Busson predicted: 'She will resume for posterity the French genius of our age. No one has understood this epoch as well as Sarah Bernhardt. She has its enthusiasms and its follies, its whims and its passing passions; she has its feverish activity. . . . All our aspirations are her own. She is indeed our muse and our queen and the most sublime expression of our time.'

Sarah Bernhardt had been the greatest actress in the world, but she had been more. She had appeared, a star of poetry, in the midst of the age of realism, the age of Zola, and she had brought to the century which was ending, the century about to begin, a kind of enchantment which the theatre had not known since Rachel. At the moment when the theatre threatened to become mediocre, if not worse, she had brought to it everything that was most beautiful and most consoling. Réjane and la Duse had had their brilliant careers. Sarah had been not merely an actress, not merely a woman: she had been a symbol and an epitome.

Select
Bibliography

English books were published in London, French books in Paris, unless otherwise stated.

AGATE, May, *Madame Sarah* (Home & Val Thal, 1945)

ARTHUR, Sir George, *Sarah Bernhardt* (Heinemann, 1923)

BARING, Maurice, *Sarah Bernhardt* (Peter Davies, 1933)

BERNHARDT, Lysiane, *Sarah Bernhardt ma Grand'mère* (Editions du Pavois, 1945)

BERNHARDT, Sarah, *The Art of the Theatre* trans. H. J. Stenning (Bles, 1924)
   A Christmas Story translated from the French in *The Silver Fairy Book* (Hutchinson, 1895)
   Dans les Nuages:Impressions d'une Chaise (Charpentier, 1878)
   Ma Double Vie. Mémoires (Charpentier, Fasquelle, 1907)
   Petite Idole (Nilsson, 1920)

BUSSON, Dani, *Sarah Bernhardt* (Fischer, undated)

CHAMPSAUR, Félicien, *Dinah Samuel* (Ollendorff, 1882)

CLAMENT, Clément, *Sarah Bernhardt. Ses Débuts – Sa Vie* (Derveaux, 1879)

COLOMBIER, Marie, *Les Mémoires de Sarah Barnum* (Chez tous les libraires, undated); translated as *The Memoirs of Sarah Barnum* (S. W. Green's Son, New York, 1884)
   Le Voyage de Sarah Bernhardt en Amerique (Dreyfous, 1882)

HAHN, Reynaldo, *La Grande Sarah. Souvenirs* (Hachette, 1930)

LANCO, Yvonne, *Belle-Île-en-Mer. Sarah Bernhardt. Souvenirs* (Nouvelles Editions Debresse, 1961)

RICHARDSON, Joanna, *Sarah Bernhardt* (Reinhardt, 1959)
   Rachel (Reinhardt, 1956)

ROSTAND, Maurice, *Sarah Bernhardt* (Calmann-Lévy, 1950)

Acknowledgments

The publishers are grateful to the following sources for providing the illustrations in this book and for giving their permission to reproduce them. Numbers in *italics* refer to colour pages.

Title page Victoria and Albert Museum
14 René Dazy
21 Bibliothèque Nationale
24–5, 28 Radio Times Hulton Picture Library
30 Roger Viollet
33, 34 Mander and Mitchenson Collection
35 Roger Viollet
36–7 Giraudon
39 Roger Viollet
41 Mansell Collection
42–3 Roger Viollet
44, 46 Mansell Collection
47 Mander and Mitchenson Collection
49 Roger Viollet
51, 52 Mander and Mitchenson Collection
54 Mansell Collection
55 Victoria and Albert Museum
58–9 Radio Times Hulton Picture Library
60 Mansell Collection
61 author
62–3 Mander and Mitchenson Collection
64 Weidenfeld and Nicolson Archive
66–7 Radio Times Hulton Picture Library
69 Victoria and Albert Museum
73 Weidenfeld and Nicolson Archive
74 Radio Times Hulton Picture Library
76 Mander and Mitchenson Collection

83 Mansell Collection
85 Ferrers Gallery (Cooper-Bridgeman Library)
86 Lords Gallery
89 Mander and Mitchenson Collection
92–3 René Dazy
95 Mander and Mitchenson Collection
97 Mansell Collection
99 René Dazy
100 Mansell Collection
101 Radio Times Hulton Picture Library
103, 104, 106 Victoria and Albert Museum
107 Mansell Collection
109 René Dazy
110 Roger Viollet
112 René Dazy
115 Radio Times Hulton Picture Library
116 Mander and Mitchenson Collection
117 Mansell Collection
119, 120 Mander and Mitchenson Collection
121 Bibliothèque Nationale
123 Mander and Mitchenson Collection
124 Mansell Collection
125 Radio Times Hulton Picture Library
126 Mansell Collection
127 Radio Times Hulton Picture Library
128 Mander and Mitchenson Collection

Index

SB = Sarah Bernhardt

Abbéma, Mlle Louise, 53, 210

Adrienne Lecouvreur (Scribe), SB performs in, 91

Adrienne Lecouvreur (Bernhardt), SB performs in, 129, 187, 221

Agar, Mme, SB performs with, 32, 35, 38

Agate, May, 20, 118, 146, 165, 186, 189, 209, 221, 222

Aiglon, L': prepared, 166–7; performed, 167, 170, 180

Alexandra, Queen, SB and, 82, 94, 202

Ambigu, Théâtre de l', SB leases, 111

America, SB visits, 95, 96, 98, 118, 144, 148, 185

Archer, William, SB criticized by, 136, 146

Arnold, Matthew, 80–1, 192

Arthur, Sir George, 88, 94, 188–9, 196

Athalie, SB performs in, 209, 212

Auber, Daniel, SB admitted to Conservatoire by, 21

Augier, Émile, SB's dislike of, 87

Austria, SB visits, 102, 131

Aventurière, L', SB performs in, 87

Aveu, L', SB performs in, 126, 129

Banville, Théodore de, SB described by, 45, 48, 87

Baring, Maurice, quoted, 57, 111, 131, 160, 197, 223, 224

Beerbohm, Sir Max, quoted, 162, 186

Belgium, SB visits, 94, 131, 148, 160

Belle-Île: described, 118; SB at, 118, 120, 122–4, 217

Bernhardt, Edouard (father of SB): described, 15, 17; dies, 18

Bernhardt, Jeanne (sister of SB), 112

Bernhardt, Lysiane (granddaughter of SB), 170, 212

Bernhardt, Maurice (son of SB): SB gives birth to, 10, 27; SB's devotion to, 27, 38, 129 and *passim*; first marriage of, 129; second marriage of, 209

Bernhardt, Mme Maurice (1) (daughter-in-law of SB), 129

Bernhardt, Mme Maurice (2) (daughter-in-law of SB), 209

Bernhardt, Régina (sister of SB), 23, 26

Bernhardt, Sarah: birth and childhood, 15–19; appearance, 9, 19–20, 45, 48, 50, 65, 82, 105 and *passim*; character, 9, 40, 45 and *passim*; theatrical achievement assessed, 9–12, 221–4 and *passim*; maternal devotion of, 27, 38, 129; illness of, 185, 189, 197, 201, 202, 203–4, 212, 216–7; death of, 217

Bernhardt, Simone (granddaughter of SB), 123, 170

Berton, Pierre: SB's liaison with, 31; 126

Biche au bois, La, SB performs in, 31

Brabender, Mlle, SB taught by, 20

Brazil, SB visits, 117–8, 185

Brohan, Augustine, 19

Burne-Jones, Sir Edward, 189

Busson, Dani, 176

Campbell, Mrs Patrick: SB described by, 216–7; SB performs with, 20, 181

Canada, SB visits, 96

Cathédrales, Les, SB performs in, 203

Champsaur, Félicien, SB described by, 108

Christian IX of Denmark, SB admired by, 94

Clairin, Georges, 118, 122

Clament, Clément, 53, 56

Claretie, Jules, SB and, 88, 89

Clemenceau, Georges, 201

Cléopâtre, SB performs in, 131

Cochran, C. B., 211–2

Colombier, Marie, 19, 53, 113

Comédie-Française: SB enters, 22, 48; SB leaves, 26, 87–8; SB's relations with, 22, 50, 68, 70, 72–3, 84, 87–8, 90

Conservatoire, SB enters, 20

Coppée, François, SB and, 32, 152

Coquelin, Constant, SB performs with, 80, 170, 174

Curie, Mme, 212

Damala, Ambroise-Aristide: early years of, 98–9; character of, 99–100; appearance of, 100; SB meets, 98; SB marries, 102; SB's life with, 111; SB's feelings for, 102, 111, 131; death of, 131

Dame aux camélias, La, SB and, 90, 96, 98, 102, 143, 148, 158, 160, 186, 222

Daniel, SB performs in, 210

D'Annunzio, Gabriele, SB and, 158

Dans les Nuages: Impressions d'une Chaise, SB writes, 70

De Max, Edouard, SB launches, 136

Denmark, SB visits, 94, 112

Dinah Samuel, SB portrayed in, 108

Double Vie, Ma, SB writes, 186

Doucet, Camille, SB and, 22, 31

Dreyfus, Captain Alfred, SB's support of, 141

Dumas, Alexandre, *père*, SB performs in play by, 31–2, 48

Dumas, Alexandre, *fils*, SB and, 61, 65, 90

Duquesnel, Félix, SB and, 31, 38, 48

Duse, Eleonora, SB's rivalry with, 111, 146, 157–9, 224

Edison, Thomas, SB visits, 96

Edward VII, SB and, 9, 82, 87, 98, 105

Egypt, SB visits, 131

Escalier, Félix, SB's *hôtel* built by, 60

Étrangère, L', SB performs in, 61, 65, 80

Eugénie, Empress, 38, 39

Fédora, SB performs in, 105, 111, 112, 136

Feuillet, Octave, SB described by, 50

Feuillet, Mme Octave, SB described by, 50

France, Anatole, 131

François le Champi, SB performs in, 31

Franco-Prussian War, 38–45

Frou-Frou, SB performs in, 91, 222, 223

Gaiety Theatre, SB performs at, 73, 78, 90, 98, 112

Garnier, Charles, 71

Garnier, Philippe, SB's liaison with, 114, 117

Gautier, Théophile: SB discussed by, 9, 68; SB describes, 68

Georges, Mlle, 21

Gismonda, SB performs in, 136, 148

Gladstone, W. E., SB's conversation with, 82, 84

Glenesk, Lord, SB's friendship with, 82, 189

Gloire, La, SB performs in, 212

Goncourt, Edmond de, 12

Grand-Champs, convent of, 19–20

Grein, J. T., 162, 165

Guitry, Lucien, SB performs with, 136, 146

Guitry, Sacha, 212

Gymnase, Théâtre du, SB at, 26–7

Hahn, Reynaldo, on SB, 120, 122, 123, 139, 157, 170, 174, 222

Hamlet, SB performs in, 160, 162

Henri, Prince de Ligne, SB's liason with, 10, 26, 31, 113

Hernani, SB performs in, 68, 223

Hollingshead, John, 73

Houdini, Harry, 205

Hugo, Victor, SB's relationship with, 9, 45–6, 68, 72

Huret, Jules, SB described by, 132–3

Iphigénie, SB makes début in, 23

Irving, Sir Henry, SB and, 77, 90, 105

Italy, SB visits, 102

Izeyl, SB performs in, 136

Jablonovska, Princess Terka: *see* Mme Maurice Bernhardt (1)

INDEX

James, Henry, SB criticized by, 65
Jarrett, William: SB meets, 72; SB
    admires, 72, 77, 90
Jeanne Doré, SB performs in, 197

Kean, ou, désordre et génie, SB performs in,
    31–2
Kératry, Comte de: SB's liaison with,
    22–3, 39, 40, 113

Lanco, Yvonne, 123, 165
Langtry, Lily: SB described by, 82; SB's
    friendship with, 82
Leighton, Sir Frederic, SB meets, 84
Lemaître, Jules, SB described by, 111
London: SB describes, 77–8, 91, 94; SB
    visits, 77–87, 90–1, 102, 118, 129, 136,
    159, 162, 176, 180, 192–3, 210–11 and
    passim
Lorenzaccio, SB performs in, 136, 148
Louÿs, Pierre, SB admired by, 126, 129

Mademoiselle de Belle-Isle, SB performs in,
    48
Maeterlinck, Maurice, 181
Magnus, Baron, SB's response to, 94
Mari qui lance sa femme, Un, SB and, 26
Marquis de Villemer, Le, SB performs in, 31
Mathilde, Princess, SB performs for, 35
Mendès, Catulle: SB asks for play by,
    111; SB described by, 148, 150, 152,
    160
Mères françaises, SB performs in, 204
Meyer, Arthur, 209–10
Mithridate, SB and, 70–1
Montesquiou, Comte Robert de, 167
Morny, Duc de, SB and, 18, 19, 22
Mounet-Sully, Jean: described, 31, 46;
    SB's liaison with, 46, 146, 160, 162
Mucha, Alphonse, 10

Nabab, Le, SB's studio inspires decor of,
    108
Nana Sahib, SB performs in, 114
Napoleon III: SB performs for, 35, 38;
    SB's affection for, 38, 39–40
Napoleon, Prince, SB and, 31
Nicholas II, Tsar, SB admired by, 148
Norway, SB visits, 131

Odéon, Théâtre de l', SB at, 31–2, 38
Oscar, King of Sweden, SB admired by,
    112

Parrot, Dr, SB attended by, 79, 80
Passant, Le, SB performs in, 32, 35, 38
Pelléas et Mélisande, SB performs in, 181
Perrin, Émile, SB and, 48, 50, 56, 57, 71,
    73, 87, 88
Petite Idole, SB writes, 129
Phèdre, SB performs in, 56–7, 78–9, 81,
    96, 136, 152
Portugal, SB visits, 102, 136
Princesse lointaine, La, SB performs in, 141,
    143, 201–2
Procès de Jeanne d'Arc, Le, SB performs in,
    186, 204
Provost, J.-B., SB taught by, 20
Punch, SB mentioned in, 81

Rachel: SB sees, 19; SB and, 11, 78, 79,
    95, 157
Régis, M., 18
Régnier, SB taught by, 20
Reine Élisabeth, La, SB performs in, 187,
    221
Réjane, SB and, 146, 160, 224
Renaissance, Théâtre de la, SB and, 136,
    148, 150
Renard, Jules, SB described by, 150
Richepin, Jean, SB's liaison with, 111,
    113
Ristori, Adelaide, 158
Rome Vaincue, SB performs in, 65, 152
Rossini, Gioacchino, 22
Rostand, Edmond: SB admired by, 141,
    152; SB in plays by, 141, 148, 157, 166
    and *passim*; SB discussed by, 117
Rostand, Maurice, 143, 144, 167, 170,
    201, 209, 212
Rueff, Suze, 56
Russia, SB visits, 102, 131
Ruy Blas, SB performs in, 45, 71–2, 223

Sainte-Sophie, Mère, 17
Samaritaine, La, SB performs in, 157
Samson, Joseph-Isidore: SB taught by,
    11, 19
Sand, George, SB's friendship with, 31
Sarah-Bernhardt, Théâtre, described,
    160, 165–6

Sarcey, Francisque, SB criticized by, 23, 45, 65, 71–2, 80, 91, 98, 157

Sardou, Victorien, SB in plays by, 105, 111, 114, 126, 131, 148, 181

Shaw, George Bernard, SB critized by, 148

Sibour, Monseigneur, 17–18

Sorcière, La, SB performs in, 181

Spain, SB visits, 102

Sphinx, Le, SB performs in, 48, 50

Sweden, SB visits, 112, 131

Switzerland, SB visits, 102

Terry, Ellen: SB's friendship with, 9, 189, 192–3; SB described by, 105, 90, 160

Théâtre-Français, 10, 23 and *passim*

Théodora, SB performs in, 114, 117

Thierry, Edmond, SB lectured by, 22

Tosca, La, SB performs in, 126, 129, 185, 186

Turkey, SB visits, 131

Van Hard, Judith (mother of SB): appearance and character of, 15; gives birth to SB, 15; lack of interest in SB, 15, 16, 17, 18, 19, 20, 22, 26, 27, 38

Victoria, Queen, SB received by, 98, 188

Voyante, La, SB performs in, 212

Wales, Prince of: *see* Edward VII

Wales, Princess of: *see* Alexandra, Queen

Walewski, Comte Alexandre, 22

Walkley, A. B., SB discussed by, 88, 189

Wilde, Oscar, SB admired by, 77, 82, 189

Wolff, Albert, SB criticized by, 84